The Profitable Retailer

*56 surprisingly simple and effective
lessons to boost your sales and profits*

By Doug Fleener

with Patricia Luebke

www.AcanthusPublishing.com
Boston

Acanthus Publishing,
a division of The Ictus Group LLC

Publisher's Cataloging-In-Publication Data
(Prepared by The Donohue Group, Inc.)

Fleener, Doug.
The profitable retailer : 56 surprisingly simple and effective lessons to boost
your sales and profits / by Doug Fleener ; with Patricia Luebke.

p. : ill. ; cm.
ISBN: 1-933631-26-0

1. Retail trade--United States--Handbooks, manuals, etc. 2. Stores, Retail--United
States--Management. 3. Small business--United States--Management. 4. Success
in business--United States--Handbooks, manuals, etc. I. Luebke, Patricia. II.
Title.

HF5429.3 .F55 2005
658.8/7

Printed in the United States of America
10 9 8 7 6 5 4 3 2 1

Layout and Inside Design by Julie Reilly
Cover and Illustrations by Charisse L. Brookman

To my father, my first retail hero.

To my mother, who encouraged me with love through all the ups and downs.

To my wife, Carin, who became a retailer by marriage and is a darn good one at that.

And to my daughters, Kate and Jane, you teach me simple and effective lessons for living every day.

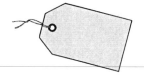

Table of Contents

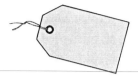

Preface

Retail. Once it's in your blood, it never leaves. Some people try it and run away as if they're being chased by a swarm of bees. They think working long hours, nights, and weekends is a problem. But that just means they're not real retailers. People don't understand why customers line up at stores at 6 a.m. the morning after Thanksgiving. They feel bad for the storeowners and managers who have to come in to work an hour before that. But then, they're not real retailers. It's either in your blood or not.

My first job was in retail; I had just turned sixteen when I was hired to work in the stationery department of a regional mass merchandiser, Turnstyle, which is no longer in business. I remember I was so proud when they gave me my blue vest and pinned my nametag on me.

My first task was to build an end-cap of back-to-school supplies. Being my first end-cap, I wanted it to be perfect, so I spent a bit more time building it than my new boss had planned.

When it was done about eight hours later, I couldn't help but spend a few minutes admiring this monument to retailing I had just created. All of a sudden, I heard my boss roar loudly,

"Fleener, I have never, ever had anyone take so long to build an end-cap. From now on I'm calling you Flash Fleener." Of course, being a new employee and a naïve teenager, I took that as a compliment. Flash Fleener did sound like a retail superhero. I was picturing it as I stood there.

Faster than a speeding shopping cart! Unloading trucks and stocking shelves in a blue-vested blur, it's Flash Fleener to the retail rescue!

Shaking me from my haze was my manager, Bruce, who said, "Come on, Flash, we've got a ton of work to do." From that day forward, retail was in my blood.

The good news is that I learned to build end-caps – and to work a price gun – faster than a quick-draw sheriff. I went on to work my way up to store management in regional and national chains. Like many, I worked retail while going to college. I tried to leave retail more than a few times, but the call of the stores always brought me back.

While in my late twenties, I eventually achieved most every retailer's dream: owning my own store. I opened a marine supply store in Jupiter, Florida, and it was the happiest day of my life. It was incredibly exhilarating getting the store ready to open – painting the walls, building the shelves, and merchandising the store. I remember I was beaming the day they hung the sign out front. It was official; I was now a storeowner.

It all went downhill from there.

I failed miserably. Like many small business owners, I was undercapitalized and spent money on the wrong things. There's an old saying, "Never confuse passion with knowledge" – and I had plenty of passion. Even after I sold my store, I wasn't about to quit retail. It was in my blood.

Many years later, two things have changed.

First, I was determined to match my experience and knowledge with my passion. I became a student of retail. While others shop to buy, I shop to learn. And where others ask questions about products, I ask people about their businesses. I don't always have an answer, but I always have a question. I never stop learning from those who do it well.

Second, I became a successful retailer. What I didn't know about running my own business, I learned working for someone else.

After selling my store, I went to work for The Sharper Image™. There I learned the importance of setting high standards and engaging the customer with products.

From there I went to work for Bose Corporation. When I started in the retail division they had one store. After opening several stores with them, I then became the first district manager. I eventually became Director of Retail, responsible for one hundred stores. Believe me, I made plenty of mistakes, and while I didn't always have the answers, I got better and better at asking the right questions. The best part is that my learning finally caught up with my passion.

Today, I help retailers of all sizes be successful. How? By asking the right questions. By sharing answers. And most importantly, by helping people achieve their dreams and the success they deserve. *Retail: once it's in your blood, it's there to stay.*

This book is an accumulation of what I've learned about what it takes to be better than the rest, a Profitable Retailer. I want to thank all the real teachers in my life including Bruce, Keith, Brian, Brad, Meg, Laurie, David, Bill W., and thousands of others.

I want to thank my family who encouraged and believed in me, even when I didn't believe in myself. I especially want to thank my wonderful wife Carin. She is a great wife, a terrific mother, and an awesome editor. But most of all, I want to thank you the reader for taking the time to read this book and for sharing with me your valuable time. I appreciate the opportunity to share this experience with you.

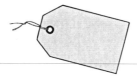

Introduction

Retail is very simple. It's the selling of goods in small quantities to the end user. But *retailing* is far from simple. It requires licenses, a location, fixtures, the buying of product, pricing it appropriately, merchandising it, hiring a staff, training that staff, then paying the staff, paying invoices and bills, and – hopefully – paying yourself.

But wait, that's just the start. Don't forget you need to buy cleaning supplies, pricing supplies, office supplies, and bags. But you're not close to opening the store yet. You need to market, advertise, and create promotions. And then you need to go to the bank, count the till, vacuum the carpet, clean the windows, restock the shelves, and unlock the doors.

Oh yeah, the most important part: the customers. You need to welcome them, answer their questions, answer the phone, take a return, clean up a mess, and – most importantly of all – make the sale.

And at the end of the day, you need to count the till, make out the deposit, lock the store, and go home to get some sleep, so you can come back and do it all over again. And if you're like many small retailers, all this has to be done by you, the owner. Yup, pretty simple, huh?

Our challenge as retailers is that we're so busy running our stores, we don't have time to run our businesses. (I define *running the store* as performing the tasks necessary to be in business and *running the business* as the strategies and plans necessary to be successful.) To achieve long-term success you, the owner, must find the time to run your store *and* run your business.

Time is a precious commodity for all of us. Besides having a business to run, most of us also juggle families, spouses, children, hobbies, civic involvement, and a host of other everyday events. Who has time to plan? Or learn? The bigger issue: Who can afford not to?

This book is written specifically for you, the overworked, overextended independent retailer. It's written with the understanding that you're busy and you don't have a lot of time to read about theories or case studies. It assumes that you're already a retailer. This is not another how-to retail book; there are plenty of those. Instead, this is a collection of lessons I've learned, if you want to sell more products, be a better marketer, make more money, and live a more comfortable life.

If you're looking for easy answers, this book is not for you. If retail success could be distilled from a single book, then every store would be wildly successful, or none of them would, since everyone would be trying to be a retailer. The fact is that no one will know your business better than you. The goal of this book is to offer up new perspectives, ask questions, and stimulate *your* thinking so you expand your mind, your sales, and your profits.

A couple of tips for using this book:

- **Never read it without a pen.** It's likely the best idea will not come from the book itself but something you think of while reading the book. Write down your thoughts while you read. (Unless it's a library book!)

- **Be open-minded.** Some of the strategies or ideas may either sound too simple to work or too complicated to try. It's my belief and hope that neither is the case, but give each one ample consideration.

In the pages that follow you will find many ideas and thoughts on ways to increase your sales and profits. I hope you're already doing many of them. I would be quite concerned if all of these were new ideas. It doesn't take but one or two of these to have a very positive impact on your profits.

Without further ado, let's dive in and put you on your path to becoming a Profitable Retailer.

Strategy

A strategy is your game plan.
In this case, it's how you're
going to go about becoming and
staying profitable. Profitable Retailers
rely on winning strategies to form
the foundation of their success.

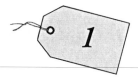

The Path to Profitability

You might have the best-looking store or the busiest. You might have the best location or the best employees. You might have the store with the most inventory or the best customer service. Even better, you might have the store with the best customer experiences. When all is said and done, there are as many ways to be successful in retail as there are retail concepts.

But there's only one way to be a *Profitable* Retailer, and that's by selling enough product or services to cover the cost of your goods and expenses and have money left over.

I'm sure you're thinking, "Duh, of course that's the only way to be profitable." You would be amazed, though, at the number of retailers I meet who don't know if they are profitable or not. I actually once heard someone say that he was "successful," but that he didn't "make any money."

Call me crazy, but I believe that the only way to measure success is to measure profits.

We retailers work incredibly hard. Like it or not, we often leave home early in the morning and come home late at night, and we often miss family events, all in the name of running our stores.

We deserve a return on that hard work. We work hard to create profits. We risk family savings to go into business. We risk losing investments from family and friends. We mortgage our homes and our futures to open our stores. We deserve a return on that risk. We take that risk to create profits.

Many retailers I meet have opened a store because of a hobby or interest of theirs. Maybe they enjoy a certain craft and feel their community is underserved in that hobby. Maybe they enjoy cooking and want to share that interest with others. If you're one of these retailers, then consider yourself blessed. You're more likely to be successful if you're knowledgeable and passionate about what you sell.

Then again, you may be more likely to fail if it's your hobby as well. Too many people run their store as a hobby rather than as a business. If it's a hobby, then call it a hobby. But if you're going to have a store, then you're a retailer, and you should run it as such. It's a hobby when you do it at home – it's a profession when you do it in a store. As a professional, the goal is to be profitable and grow your business.

Becoming a Profitable Retailer allows us to do many of the things we've dreamed about. We can be self-employed and not have to have a boss or do the corporate "rah rah" thing. We can travel more often, own a bigger home, or eventually, have the opportunity to spend more time with family and friends. Most important, building a profitable store or chain can give us financial security and peace of mind.

But it all starts with one simple idea: you have to bring in more money than you spend. Simply said, not simply done. It begins with the mindset that you deserve and will achieve profitability. As a former client of mine always says, "Our businesses don't fail us, but rather we fail our business." The rest of this book is about you becoming a Profitable Retailer, creating the profits and success you deserve and can achieve.

The Question: Are you ready to be a more Profitable Retailer?

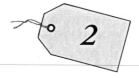

All Retail is Local

Being an independent Profitable Retailer in today's super-center world is not easy. Large and ever-expanding discount chains are threatening small retailers around the globe. One of the myths of retail is that these chains are killing all the independent stores. The fact is that the chains are killing off the *weak* independents while the strong are learning to leverage the competition.

Remember this: all retail ultimately is *local*. Regardless of where your competitor's corporate office is or where they get their products, everyone has to compete in the *local* market. And it's how well you compete that ultimately determines your level of profitability. Yes, it's likely you won't have the lowest prices, but with the right business model, that's fine. But you better be the best at something or profits will be difficult to obtain.

Profitable Retailers know that they aren't going to out-Wal-Mart Wal-Mart®. Wal-Mart is almost always going to have lower prices than you. Profitable Retailers, however, learn to find unique products and niches that Wal-Mart, Target®, and other discounters don't have. Profitable Retailers may also differentiate themselves by offering their customers a higher level of service with a more engaging and expert staff.

Your customer is local. Your employees are local. And the opportunity for success is local. Who better understands what your customers want than you? Who can better create relationships with organizations, schools, and other small businesses than you? All retail is local, and you can use that as your competitive advantage. Here are three tips:

Get locally involved. Join the Chamber of Commerce. Be active in local groups such as the Lions, the Elks, or the Knights of Columbus. Work closely with local charities. Make your name and face synonymous with your store.

Build local alliances. Create alliances with businesses that share the same customer base as you. This is especially beneficial when you're planning a direct mail or email advertising campaign and you want to drive new customers to your store. By building relationships with the right companies, you may be able to access their customers' addresses, emails, and phone contact information.

Sponsor local events. Invite local clubs and associations to host their meetings in your store. Let one of the high school bands, drama groups, or choirs hold a performance. Advertise your events and promote them to the teeth. Provide free drinks and food. It works for coffee shops and pubs – why not you?

You're local, *your* business is local, and done right, *your* profits are local.

The Question: Are you leveraging your local connections to beat your competition?

Differentiate – or Else

A toy store in my town recently went out of business and the owner was quite bitter, blaming the town, the residents, and anyone else he could name. I think if we still had a milkman, he'd blame him, too.

The fact is, he didn't offer enough of a difference in products and services to differentiate himself from Target and Wal-Mart. Remember this: If a customer can't differentiate a retailer, she will always base purchase decisions on price, and that doesn't bode well for independents.

The retail landscape is littered with "me too" retailers. Profitable Retailers know that differentiating themselves is even more critical to independent retailers. They know each day that customers *make a decision* to do business with them or not. Clearly communicating to the customer what makes them different from the competitors enables them to achieve the sales volume necessary to be profitable. Sound like a strategic competitive advantage? Exactly. You can now see how they all fit together.

So how do you differentiate yourself? It's really not as hard as it sounds. Just apply three easy steps.

Step #1: Differentiate what you sell. Carrying the same exact product mix as the discounters can be retail suicide for an independent. You will be more profitable when you offer your customers products that are unique and different from your competitor. Finding different products is easier said than done, but it is vital to your success. You might specialize in a certain niche – perhaps handmade or imported goods – and offer a broader depth of selection in that area than your competition.

The toy store I referred to earlier could have done a number of things to differentiate their products. They could have specialized in board games. Another possibility would have been to create custom birthday and holiday toy baskets determined by a child's age and interest – something that isn't offered by others. Now you're not just selling goods, you're offering a service as well.

Step #2: Offer your customers a different experience. Most retailers focus on what they sell rather than the customer they sell it to. Focusing on and involving the customer can greatly differentiate a retailer's store from the competition. When a customer feels good about his shopping experience, he is likely to return again and tell family and friends.

Our toy store owner could have hosted free classes on how to play chess and other board games. Maybe he could have worked with charity groups to offer shopping nights where the charity received a portion of the revenue. (We'll explore more of these ideas later in the book.) In the ultra-competitive toy business, he might have to find a hundred of these ideas, but each of these ideas separates him from the competition and creates loyal customers. It's not easy, but no one said being a Profitable Retailer would be.

Step #3: Communicate your points of differentiation.
Once you've determined how you're different, you need to
communicate that difference to current and potential customers.
Too many retailers simply advertise products and don't let
customers know what makes their store different and unique.
You'll read more about this in the marketing chapter.

Let's take one last look back to the now-defunct toy store. Since
there was nothing unique about what he sold or what took place
in his store, his advertising wasn't effective either. One more
element that led to his demise. One more store littering the "me
too" highway.

The Question: What is different about your store? How does
the customer see these differences? How do you tell customers
about the differences?

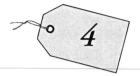

Know Your Competition
as You Know Thyself

You can't leverage or beat your competitors if you don't know who they are. Profitable Retailers know their competitor is not always who it may appear to be. It may or may not be a large chain store. It may or may not be another store like yours. The competition could also be other types of businesses that compete for the same consumer dollars.

For example: My consulting firm once worked with the owner of a paint-your-own pottery store. A large percentage of her revenue came from hosting children's birthday parties. We helped her realize that her competition is not just other paint-your-own pottery stores, but also other businesses that offer birthday parties – everyone from Chuck E Cheese® to the local bowling alley to the gymnastics center.

You can't beat them if you don't identify them.

Once you know who your competitors are, you need to know what they're doing. After identifying the "birthday party" competition, my client could then look at all of the options that were available to a parent booking a party. Now she could put together her points of differentiation (a big point being that the kids get to keep what they create forever) and communicate those to her customers. (As a side note, we discovered that one of the keys to selling parties is to make life easy for mom and dad.)

Finally, learn from your competition. In a *Wall Street Journal* article about the launch of Tommy Hilfiger's then-new "H Hilfiger" collection, an apparel analyst with Goldman Sachs said a challenge to designers is to take what they learn from local retailers and designers and apply it to the mass market.

Profitable Retailers do exactly the opposite. They learn from the mass market and successfully apply those lessons to the local market. When visiting Target, Costco®, or one of your large competitors, what do you see them doing that you can do?

For example: Dollar stores and dollar areas have become quite popular with mass merchandisers but independent retailers have been slow to adopt the idea. The retailers who have embraced this concept have increased their impulse purchase sales, thereby increasing their overall sales and profits.

Staying on top of what your local and national competitors are doing is critical. You need to make sure you find the time to get out of the store and go shopping. You need to visit your competitors at least once each quarter, if not more often. While in the stores, ask questions. Employees will give you an amazing amount of information if you just ask. Then ask yourself what they're doing right, what they could do better, and the most important question, what you've learned so you can do better.

Many retailers feel uncomfortable shopping their local competitors. As one client told me, "I can't go in there – they know me." Sure you can. There's nothing wrong with visiting your competition and talking shop. Some of my best friends are my competitors. Of course I make sure to take a peek or two when I'm in the store visiting – just to see what they are selling or how they are displaying products.

Another great and simple way to stay on top of your competition: create an online news alert. This is very easy to do. Go to Google™ or any other news and search engine site and set up an alert. These are email updates you receive daily or weekly (depending on your preference) with the latest news on whatever term, topic, or subject you want to monitor.

Define your search to include a national competitor's name, a product category, or anything else you deem important (celebrity gossip, baseball scores, etc.). Every time an article, press release, filing, or blog entry appears on that topic, you'll receive an email with a link to the source of the information. Click on the link and it will take you right there.

You can't beat the competition if you don't know what they're doing. Setting up a news alert is probably the easiest way to get the inside scoop.

The Question: Who's your competition? What do they do well? What don't they do well?

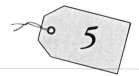

To Thine Own Customer Be True

Recently my friends and I were talking about the fear of rejection and rejection itself. Naturally, each of us could tell our own tales of rejection.

I can send out an email newsletter to thousands of people, and if one person unsubscribes, I feel rejected. Of course, I'm failing to recognize all of the people who probably enjoyed the newsletter and took something away from it. As a speaker, I'll often focus on the one person in the audience who seems uninterested in my speech rather than the rest of the audience, who may be entirely engaged with the topic.

As retailers, we are often challenged by this same fear of rejection. Every day, we want every single customer who walks in the store to like us. No, not just *like* us. We want our customers to *love* us so much that they spend lots of money with us.

Unfortunately, it's impossible to have every person who walks in our store become our customer. It's not only impossible but it's bad business. That may sound like retail blasphemy, but the simple fact is: you can't have every person who walks in the door become your customer. Lack of focus has been the downfall of many un-Profitable Retailers.

As diverse as we all look based on our size, shape, and skin color, so too are people diverse in their life experiences and needs. Some consumers are incredibly frugal, going far out of their way to save a few pennies. Others demand a high level of service at practically any price. Whatever we sell, it's going to be a "must have" for some and "no need to have" for others.

The fact is: we *should* be rejected by those we are not targeting. It doesn't mean that we can't deliver an excellent store experience, but they may not need or desire our products. Rejection is a good thing as it means we are not trying to be all things to all people. To be a Profitable Retailer, it's important to know who is and isn't rejecting you.

Consider a retailer who sells medium- to high-end purses. Many women who come into that store may not be able to afford to spend hundreds of dollars on a purse. Even if they can afford it, they may have no desire to spend that much money on a handbag. Those people may look around a bit and even comment to a friend how "overpriced" the purses are. When we hear these comments we become defensive, maybe even resentful.

What *is* important is for us to question whether they are knowledgeable buyers or not. If they are within our targeted customer base, why do they believe the purses are overpriced? If they are not within our targeted customer base, what they are actually saying is that they either can't afford the purse or choose not to spend that much on a purse. Of course the retailer should take the opportunity to educate them and create potential customers. With a little education you may move your customers from thinking your product is overpriced to becoming something they aspire to own.

Too much rejection is a bad thing. It means no profits. When too many customers reject your products and store it could mean that your strategy is wrong. I once met a woman who had a terrific concept, the product selection was unique, the experience differentiated, and the store was gorgeous. There was only one problem: too many customers rejected her. They didn't buy. The store was too up-market for the community. She either needed to move her store or change her product mix to something more affordable for her customer.

Rejection from a non-buyer of our products is only natural. We could in the future sell lower-priced purses, but if we do we run the risk of alienating our targeted customers. If we are rejected by someone in our targeted customer base, we need to find out why. Remember, all rejections are not created equal.

Don't be offended when you overhear comments of rejection, but take the time to learn from the customers. Ask them questions to better understand what they have bought in the past. Find out where else they shop. Learn everything you can about these customers and use it to shape and evolve your strategy.

In our lives and in our stores, rejection is an everyday part of life. What's important is knowing when to accept it or not. And as Shakespeare once said, "to thine own self be true." The sentiment applies to retail, too. To thy targeted customer be true; thank you and goodbye to the rest.

The Question: Are you willing to confront your own feelings of rejection?

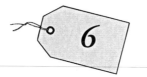

Try Once. Measure Twice.
Count Your Profits.

Carpenters have a saying: "Measure twice, cut once." Profitable Retailers measure and track key metrics that are critical to their businesses. Many retailers only track daily sales, but traffic and transaction counts are just as important as other measurements that are more specific to your retail segment. Traffic counting is one of the most underutilized measurements in retail. Counting *transactions* helps a retailer measure conversions but counting *traffic* will help you measure opportunities.

The only ways to increase sales are to either sell more to the people already coming into your store or bring more people to your store. Tracking dollars per traffic and dollars per transaction will help you determine if new marketing or presentation strategies are effective or not. It makes no sense to spend hundreds (or thousands) of dollars on an advertising campaign and then not have any way of knowing if the ad is working.

How about when you run a coupon in a Valpak®-style mailing? Do you track the returns of those? When the Valpak sales rep shows up again (and you know he will) you need to make your decision about running another coupon based on solid numbers and not just a feeling of "It worked pretty well," or "We didn't get many."

It's not just advertising or traffic you need to track. From time-to-time, you may buy some merchandise believing that it's going to be your next hot seller, only to be disappointed with the results. Well, before you declare it your newest "dog" of a purchase, try making some changes. Move it to a different location in the store. Consider some different signage or lighting. Review the pricing. Oftentimes it's not the product that's not working, but rather the presentation.

As you're tracking your numbers, don't forget to include some side notes on factors that may have impacted those numbers.

For example: If the street in front of your store is being repaved, your numbers for that week may be way down. The same if there was a blizzard or power failure. On the positive side, a great article about your store in the local paper, Valentine's Day, or other holiday may positively impact your sales.

One of the best ways to track your data is to create a store log. You can either do it manually or on your computer. It's almost like a store diary. Track your tests, thoughts, and comments on what worked and didn't work in the log. Over time it can be a great resource for you to reference. As a holiday or season approaches, you can read what was done the year before and not have to rely on just your memory.

One of the advantages of being a Profitable Retailer is that you also get to measure and track profits!

The Question: Is your system for tracking sales accurate and useful?

"Investing" in Your Store and Yourself

"I'm too busy running the store to do all those other things I know I need to get done," a storeowner recently told me.

This certainly wasn't the first time I've heard this lament from a retailer. I've heard it from clients I've worked with one-on-one as well as audience members at my presentations. Those "other things" often include marketing, recruiting, business planning, reviewing financial documents, etc. As owners, we're so busy running the store that we don't have time to run the business.

I usually respond by recommending that the owner consider adding a part-time employee or two to free up time to do these important "other things." Almost without fail the person replies, "I can't afford that." The fact is that you can't afford not to. It's vital that the owner of a business has time to focus on the elements of the business that will make it successful. Most of us only need about four or five hours a week of focused and uninterrupted time to spend on these "other things." Some may see the extra payroll only as an added expense.

I believe it's an *investment*.

Here's a great example. Every year when spring comes around, my thumb slowly turns black. I am the Dr. Kevorkian of lawn care. No matter what I do, the crabgrass wins, the critters build condos underground, and I end up frustrated, hot, and sweaty. So I went back to hiring a lawn service. I used a lawn service up until I started my own company. Then I decided I shouldn't spend approximately $120 per month on yard maintenance.

At first I saw the $120 as an expense. I now realize that by investing in the lawn service, I have an additional five to six hours each month to market my company, time that could result in a speaking or consulting engagement that nets considerably more than the investment in the lawn service. It also keeps me from having to handle fertilizer; I can spend more time with my family, and I get real grass that's free of critters. Of course I could choose to take care of the lawn myself and pay someone else to market my business, but I don't believe that's the best use of my time. Like the owner of a store, I can delegate many things, but the key to my business' success is to personally focus on those important "other things."

So the next time you find that you don't have time to do those "other things," do what other Profitable Retailers do. Stop and consider if the cost to find the time is an expense or an investment. I've found that by investing in the appropriate help, I'm happier, more profitable, and best of all, my yard is no longer the most depressing sight in the neighborhood.

The Question: Would additional help free you up for more important work?

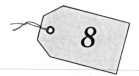

Hurry Up and Change

Has this ever happened to you? You have an idea that you're sure will have a positive impact on your store's sales. You've been thinking about this idea for months; now it's time to act.

The idea requires an investment in new signage, changes in some on-floor processes, and the necessary staff training. You contact your graphic designer to begin work on the sign. You start mapping out your new process and begin working on the necessary PowerPoint training.

Forty-five days later you roll out your new strategy and it seems to be well received by employees and customers alike. After ninety days, you're pleased to see that your sales have improved by three percent. You attribute the increased sales to your new strategy.

Now that you've proven your concept, you decide to roll the strategy into your other stores. You wish all your tests and new concepts went this smoothly.

The problem is that it went too smoothly. It took forty-five days to test it and ninety days more to consider it a success. In that same period of time you could have tested multiple variations of the same strategy, which may well have generated *considerably more* than the three percent growth you've achieved.

Tom Kelley, General Manager of the world-famous and widely admired design and development firm IDEO and author of *The Art of Innovation*, encourages companies to "Fail often to succeed sooner."*

As Profitable Retailers, we improve our stores through trial and error. We beat our competitors through speed, innovation, differentiation, and execution. We succeed because we test, we fail, we learn, and we improve. We will improve our stores by doing more imperfect tests.

Profitable Retailers know that ideas without action are just that – ideas. Ideas alone won't improve your business; rather, testing and implementing them does. To be innovative, we must learn to live with less than ideal situations in our tests. If we wait for perfect conditions, we may miss our window of opportunity. Imperfect tests mean we may use fixtures that don't match, signage that's less than ideal, trainings created on the fly, and measurements that may be challenging to extrapolate. We must remember we are often testing a concept and not necessarily the execution. Validate the concept or idea and then you can execute the solution appropriately.

Okay. Now take the above example and see what happens when you emphasize speed and innovation over perfect testing.

- After thinking about your idea for a day or so, you decide to run a quick test. You gather your team and tell them what you're thinking. Together you brainstorm

---

* Tom Kelly. *The Art of Innovation*. New York: Currency, 2001. p. 232.

how to change the signage and what they will need to do differently.

- You stop at Kinko's on your way to work the next morning and pick up your cheaply made signs. True, they don't look nearly as good as your regular signs but it's an imperfect test. Get over it! I would use cardboard for a few days if it helped me prove or disprove my concept.

- You implement your new strategy in your store. (If you own several, pick one and test it out there first.)

- After a few days, you gather the staff to get their feedback on the new strategy. It's decided that the signage is working fine, but the process needs tweaking. After another few days, your staff tells you that this new strategy improves the customer experience and is having a positive impact on sales. Your retail instincts and experience tell you it's a winner and to go with it.

- You bring in the graphic designer to improve the signs. Your staff helps map out the new process and create the new training. You're ready to roll the new strategy into all your stores.

The perfect test took nearly six months from concept to rollout. The imperfect test took fewer than twenty-eight days.

John Kotter, Harvard professor and author of *Leading Change*, says that producing change is eighty percent leadership and twenty percent management.*

---

* John Kotter, "Winning at Change." *Leader to Leader*. No. 10, Fall 1998. http://drucker.org/leaderbooks/L2L/fall98/kotter.html

As a Profitable Retailer, you must be willing to lead your organization through innovation and imperfect testing. As a leader, you must not only be willing to try new things, you must be willing to fail. Most important, you must refuse to stand still. Any retailer not moving forward is moving backward. The time to change is now. The time to innovate is now.

The Question: What idea or change have you thought about that you can begin now?

9

The Lifetime Value ($$$) of a Customer

Does it drive you crazy when a customer complains and you end up taking a product back or writing off the cost of repair in order to keep that customer happy?

Customers can be maddening, but Profitable Retailers know that they need to build a solid base of loyal, repeat customers as opposed to focusing on short-term results.

Question: Have you ever estimated what a loyal customer is worth in sales over her lifetime, if she keeps coming back to your store? For example: A national pizza operator has estimated the average "lifetime sales value" of a loyal customer is around $13,000. Do you think they mind having to give away a pizza or two in order to keep a customer happy?

For a high-end hotel operator such as Ritz-Carlton, the lifetime sales value of a loyal guest may be well over $100,000. With that amount of money at stake, the hotel staff would have no problem spending $2,000 to keep a guest happy – no questions asked.

So how do you figure the lifetime value of your customer? There are many formulas, some of which are better suited for individuals with PhDs in statistics.

However, here's one simple formula to give you an idea.

- Start with the average purchase of a customer. (Example: $100)

- Then take the number of times that customer buys from you during the year. (Example: Five purchases)

- Multiply those two numbers together and you get your customer's yearly average value. (Example: $500)

- Now figure out how many years a typical customer stays with you. This is what we mean by "lifetime." "Lifetime" doesn't mean literally. Some stores – a jewelry store perhaps – may have customers who last a lifetime, while other customers' "lifetimes" may be a few years. One grocery store chain figures that the lifetime for a customer is ten years. (For our example, let's say the customer shops with you for seven years.)

- Multiply this yearly average by your customer's "lifetime" and you get a *lifetime value for the customer.* (In our example, $3,500)

Calculating the lifetime value of a customer isn't just an academic exercise. When you know the lifetime value of a particular customer, you'll know what request is reasonable for you to respond to.

For example: If you know the lifetime value of a customer is $7,000, you will be able to satisfy that customer – oftentimes gladly – rather than resent every request the customer makes. Letting this customer return a product you may not be able to return yourself doesn't seem so bad now that you think of the $7,000 in sales you'll eventually get from him.

Profitable Retailers know it always costs less to keep a customer than it does to find a new one. Look at your customers in terms of their long-term sales potential – if they keep coming back again and again – not just what they may spend on one visit to your store. Communicate this concept to your staff and enlist their ideas and support in finding ways to turn casual customers into loyal ones.

The Question: What is the lifetime value of a typical customer of yours? And do your employees understand the lifetime value of a typical customer?

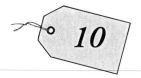

"Fear Factor" – Retail-Style

After a speaking engagement, I always like to meet and talk with retailers in the audience. I enjoy hearing their feedback and how what I said that day related to their own stores and particular situations.

Following one recent talk, I was approached by a woman who had a few questions for me. While talking with her, it became clear that she has some wonderful business opportunities for her store, but has been held back from taking advantage of them. She has access to the necessary capital. She has the knowledge and skills. And she is positive that the business opportunity is there.

The only thing holding her back is her own fear.

Fear itself is defined as "an emotion experienced in anticipation of some possible or probable situation or event." It may be the fear of failing. Or it might be the fear of success. It could be the fear of losing one's investment. It even could be the fear of making too much money. Fear keeps us from moving forward and achieving our dreams. Of course, fear can also be healthy and prevent us from doing things that are either dangerous or ill-planned.

As the woman and I continued to talk, we discussed the fact that the biggest obstacle to achieving her goal was her own low tolerance for risk. Clearly she was fearful either of the risk necessary to be successful or of her own abilities.

Without risk there can be no reward. The ability to take on and manage risk is in the DNA of every Profitable Retailer. If not, you wouldn't open a store but would work for someone else or not work at all. Fear of your own abilities is often a lack of confidence. Many of us were told at some point in our lives that we couldn't do something or we would never be as good as someone else. Those are old tapes playing in our heads and are creating the fear inside ourselves. Erase them! You can achieve any goal you set with hard work and the right knowledge and skills.

I suggested that this woman needed to take a hard look at her fears and determine what was holding her back. Maybe her fear was protecting her, or maybe her fear was nothing more than a simple fear of change. (Funny how we'll stay in an uncomfortable or unsuccessful situation because change – any change – can be difficult.)

In this case, I advised her to write a small business plan so that she could take a look at the opportunities from a rational and unemotional viewpoint. From there, she'll be able to make a decision on whether to grow her business or not.

Don't be held back by thinking that writing a small business plan is too complex. Maybe you'll want to write a standard business plan, or maybe you'll simply want to make a list of pros and cons, followed by a projected budget and timeline. Think about best-case and worst-case scenarios. Explore your idea in writing and take it out of the deep, dark, scary arena and into the rational and businesslike light of day.

It's okay to not grow your business or take that next promotion, especially if you're risk-averse. Your own fears might be protecting you. More often than not though, our fears are holding us back. It's important to know what is behind your fear so that you can manage the risk and reward.

That's when I like to take the emotion out of my decision and make it based on solid information I possess, as well as the information I get from talking with others. When I do this, I gain the confidence and ability to move forward. Here are three easy steps to manage your fear.

Step #1: Put it down on paper. Draw a line down the middle of a sheet of paper. On the left side write down all the reasons you should do what you're considering doing. Don't try to rationalize or over think it. Just brainstorm reasons to do it. On the right side of the paper list all of the reasons you shouldn't. My guess is that left side will be practical and the right side more emotional. That's okay.

Now prioritize the top three on each side. Consider the risk and reward of each. Look at your right side priorities and think about what you could do to move them to the left side. As an example, you may have written that you don't understand marketing enough to support a growing business. That's a healthy fear. It's also something that can be easily overcome by signing up for classes at a local college or reading a few books.

After you've made your list, write out a short plan like the woman I met did. It doesn't have to be elaborate. You can do it on the computer or on paper. What's important is that you think your change through to identify what will be needed to achieve success.

Step #2: Talk with a friend or mentor. I find when we

share our fears that they have less power over us. Share your list of why you should or shouldn't make the change you're considering. I would recommend that if it's business-related, you try to find someone impartial and knowledgeable about your business. While it's important to have your family involved, they may not be impartial. While you will definitely need to involve them before you make a final decision, a mentor or coach is a better resource at this point in your decision making.

Step #3: Make a decision. I have learned from my own personal experience that making the decision is more agonizing than the outcome of the decision. You've gathered your data, you've talked with another person, and now it's time to move forward. If at this point fear is holding you back, there lies your decision. If you decide to move forward, you now know you have done due diligence and have put yourself in position to be a more Profitable Retailer.

When an opportunity is before them, Profitable Retailers make a decision to act or not, and leave fear behind. All of us deserve success, but we have to take some risks to achieve it.

The Question: What fear is holding you back?

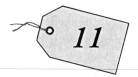

Enjoy Those Hard-Earned Profits!

The end result of any retailer's strategy is profits. With profits come security, peace of mind, and the ability to help others and enjoy our lives. Retailing is not easy. It usually requires long hours and hard work, but Profitable Retailers find it quite satisfying. Connecting with customers and developing relationships with them is a gratifying way to spend a day.

Your store is your home, and your home is your store. You get restless on vacations and cut them short for work. Sleep and leisure time feel like a waste. If this describes you, watch out. You may be working too hard and not getting the time away necessary to be successful.

Working hard may seem like a good thing, and it is, but doctors cite excessive work and worrying about work as contributing factors to stress, hypertension, ulcers, and insomnia. Running a store is a demanding business, and anyone who's lazy should not be there in the first place. But that doesn't mean immersing yourself in work to the point of excluding everything else. To make sure you're enjoying your profits, try some of the following methods:

Reserve "free time." When at work, take at least a few minutes to call someone who's special to you and don't talk business. Then, when you go home, enjoy time for yourself and with your loved ones. Wait until the morning to resume the pace of work. Use your vacation time for what it's supposed to be – a vacation!

Take care of your body. Join a gym. Ride a bicycle. Jog around the neighborhood. Storeowners don't get paid sick days. If your health fails, who's going to mind the store?

Try new things. Even when not using your leisure time, Profitable Retailers can break out of a rut by using a daily schedule to do new things. Join a local business association or civic club. Attend a convention or trade show. Read a good book, whether it's about business or not. Think of it as a way to fill your head with new ideas that may be useful in business, or just useful to you.

Work your plan. Re-examine your goals from time to time, Are you doing what you want with your business? With your life? Take a broad view of things and it will cause less worry about the nagging details of each day. Also, take time to reflect positively on what you've accomplished. It will give you the confidence to face your fears and take more risks.

The Question: What can you do to make sure you are enjoying your profits?

Customer Experience

 ❦

When you're trying to manage your
store, it's easy to forget that the very
reason you have a store is for your
customers. Profitable Retailers value
all customers and continually work on
ways to improve their experiences.

 ❦

It's All About the Customer – Period

Profitable Retailers know they're in business for one reason: the customer. They know exactly who the customers are, what they do, and what they want. And when the customers' tastes evolve and change, so does the product the retailer offers. Profitable Retailers know their number one priority is to serve the customers and maximize every opportunity to sell them products. They know that treating the customer with respect gives them a key strategic advantage over the competition.

It sounds like a no-brainer, but retailers seem to love to do everything but focus on the customer. Try it for yourself. Go to the mall and go into twenty stores. It doesn't matter what stores. It's likely that over half of the stores will have employees doing tasks instead of focusing on the customer. There's no reason to stock shelves or clean cases if you don't have any customers!

Profitable Retailers are profitable because their competitors are product-centric. All of their competitors' actions, all of their conversations, and everything they do is based upon what they sell. Their total identify is product-focused.

Profitable Retailers are customer-centric. Their actions are based on what their customers need. Their conversations are based on the customer they serve. Everything they do is to build a stronger relationship with their customer.

Here are five ways to become a more customer-centric Profitable Retailer:

Welcome every single customer that comes into the store.
There's nothing more important to the Profitable Retailer than making sure you acknowledge and welcome the customer into the store. First, it so rarely happens in other stores that you immediately begin to differentiate your store from others. Second, it communicates to the customers that you're focused on them and appreciate the opportunity to serve them. Third, it communicates to your employees (and reminds you!) that the customer *is your primary focus and your reason for being in business.*

Don't show the customer any products until you have asked the customer a few questions about his needs.
Just by taking time to ask questions demonstrates that you truly do want to show customers the best product that meets their needs, regardless of the price point. Making sure the customer purchases the right product reduces returns and increases customer satisfaction.

When you leave lists of things that should be done by your staff, always put "*Serve the Customer*" on the first line. There's an old saying in retail that "what gets inspected is respected." Every day your actions and comments convey to your employees what you believe is truly important. If you believe the customer is your #1 priority, and you want your employees to feel the same way, don't have them straightening racks on the sales floor when the store is busy; ask them to focus on helping the customer instead.

Don't make snide or inappropriate comments about the customer. My mother always said that if you don't have anything nice to say, don't say anything at all, which is great advice when making any comments about customers. Making snide or inappropriate comments about the customer communicates to the staff that your "we value the customer" approach is just talk.

Create a customer profile. Best Buy recently launched a customer-centric strategy that is based on four different types of customers who shop their stores. They have created archetypical customers Buzz (the Techie), Barry (Wealthy Professional), Ray (Family Man), and Jill (Soccer Mom). For each customer segment, the company has identified what in the shopping experience is important to that particular customer as well as what products and services they are likely to buy. Best Buy even merchandises a store based on which segment is the dominant group in that market.

Give your customers names. Brainstorm what is important to them. If you sell women's clothing, you may have a 35-year-old female customer, a 50-year-old female customer, and a husband. Teach your staff how to maximize each customer's experience. As a husband, I know that if I'm shopping in a women's clothing store, I'm less interested in what I buy and more concerned that my wife will like it, whatever it turns out to be. I want the process to be fast and painless, and I don't want to spend a lot of time thinking about it. This is generally not what women shopping for themselves are looking for in a shopping experience.

Customer profiles can also help you buy more efficiently, merchandise more effectively, and most important, help you and the staff remember that your number one reason for being in business is to serve your customer. And now you even know her name!

Without customers there's no need for merchandise – period. Without customers there's no need for employees – period. Without customers there are no profits – period.

One thing Profitable Retailers never forget is that it's always about the customer. Period.

The Question: Are you product-centric or customer-centric?

The Other CRM – Customer *Respect* Management

Here's a business strategy that can have a huge impact on your sales, and it doesn't require a large investment – no fancy software to buy and you don't have to hire companies to implement it. As a matter of fact, you're already doing it. The question is: are you doing it well?

This critical business tool is CRM: Customer *Respect* Management. It's different than Customer Relationship Management, which is an integration of people, process, and technology that provides seamless integration of every area of business that touches the customer. Make no mistake, Customer Relationship Management is a great strategy for large corporations that present multiple faces to the customer. But regardless of your size, scope, or business, every company needs to excel in Customer *Respect* Management.

Customers are the very foundation of why you're in business. They purchase your goods and services. Without customers, you're out of business faster than you can say, "May I help you?" Customer *Respect* Management means holding the customers in the highest esteem and having a great appreciation for them. It's not just a strategy. It's an action. It's what Profitable Retailers do on a daily basis.

Almost all companies believe they're high in Customer *Respect* Management. I wish this were the case. If it was, every time you went shopping it would be a great experience. You would leave stores feeling good about your experience. Unfortunately, as customers we more often feel under-appreciated and not respected by many of the companies we do business with. Ask a group of retail executives and owners if they respect their customers and everyone will raise their hands. Ask a group of customers if they feel respected by retailers and considerably fewer hands will go up. Actions do speak louder than words.

I have to stop here for a minute with a rant. Store owners who consciously or unconsciously allow employees to park their cars in the best spots closest to the door should be ashamed of themselves. One day I went to the Starbucks® down the street. The first four parking spaces were taken so I pulled into the fifth, walked into the store and saw four employees and no customers in the store. Shame.

The Stop & Shop® grocery store across from Starbucks is the same. When the store opens at 7 a.m., half of the parking spots nearest the doors are taken and there's not a customer in sight. Shame.

These are spaces that could be better used by the elderly, by a parent with young children in tow, or – heck! – me. I'm your customer. But no, employees who haven't been trained to respect the customers enough to walk an extra twenty to thirty steps twice a day take the best spots.

In small towns across America, including my own, retailers complain that customers don't shop in their stores due to lack of parking. All too many of those same retailers walk out and feed the meter in front of their stores so their car doesn't get a parking ticket. Shame.

Consider the lost sales from a customer who had planned to come to your store, but gave up when there was not a handy parking space. Maybe that customer had just a limited amount of time, and when he saw that no space was readily available, that customer just kept driving.

It's ironic that retailers spend millions of dollars on Customer Relationship Management when the bigger problem is Customer *Respect* Management. I would put up signs in front of all the close parking spaces that read, "Reserved for our best customer: You."

Profitable Retailers know that strong and lasting relationships of all kinds begin with respect. Customer *Respect* Management doesn't require a large investment of time or money. It just requires that you respect your employees, and then let your actions as a leader speak as loud as your words. Ensuring that your store is high in Customer *Respect* Management will guarantee a successful and lasting relationship with your customers.

The Question: What action will you take today to show a little extra *respect* to your customers?

"Welcome" – the Most Profitable Word in Retail

I'm always amazed at the number of retailers who just flat-out miss sales. Here's a case in point. My wife, Carin, went shopping for a new bicycle for our oldest daughter. We prefer to shop, when we can, at local businesses rather than the big box stores, so her first stop was a small bicycle shop in the next town.

Carin entered the store and the owner, whom she recognized from the website, was helping a customer while another employee was on the telephone. No other customers were in the store, but Carin – a potential *new* customer – didn't receive a single acknowledgment from either the owner or the employee. Not a hello. Not a nod. Not a "Welcome. When I'm finished with this customer, I'll be happy to help you."

She was totally ignored. She looked around a bit but she'd already determined that she wasn't going to spend a dime in that store.

Off she went to another bicycle shop. Here she received great service, a quality product, a fair price, and a store experience where she felt valued as a customer.

So, one store made $150 more in sales than the other one did that Friday. Big deal, right?

Well, odds are I'll buy another five bikes or so in my life, and it's obvious where I'm going to shop. So if I spend, say, $1,500 on bikes over the next eight years at forty points, ignoring my wife, just cost that first storeowner $600 gross profit. ($1,500 in gross sales *minus* cost is $600 in gross profits from the sales of the five bikes.) On average, if he ignores two customers a week, he has now lost over $60,000 of lifetime profits. All because he couldn't, or chose not to, wait on more than one customer at a time.

Profitable Retailers know there's a difference between welcoming the customer and saying "hello." To welcome someone is to receive a person warmly, while a "hello" is a simple greeting. While a "hello" is definitely better than being ignored, it can be more profitable to give each customer a hearty welcome.

Consider your own home. When someone comes into your home do you just say, "Hi, feel free to look around and if you have any questions please let me know"? Of course not. You welcome your guest and maybe give him or her a hug. Often you tell guests you're happy to see them. Now I'm not sure hugging the customer is the best strategy, but if you receive them as warmly into your store as you would your home, the results will be quite profitable.

It's important to teach your staff the value of the word "welcome." When customers are welcomed, they already feel more connected with the store and the staff, increasing the likelihood of buying something and recommending your store to family and friends.

When you greet customers, at least use the word "hello."

Discourage the use of "Hey," "Yo," "Hi," "What's up?" and other ways to improperly greet and welcome a customer.

Welcoming every single customer, a noble goal to strive for, is challenging and most likely unobtainable. In cases where you're busy with other customers, new customers can be welcomed by making eye contact, smiling, and nodding – something that would have saved the retailer my wife visited extensive profits.

Profitable Retailers know that "welcome" is the most important and profitable word in retail. And besides that, it's good manners.

The Question: Do you welcome or at least acknowledge every customer who comes into your store? If not, what's it costing you?

Quit Telling the Customer "No" to Get Them to Say "Yes"

The key to creating sales is to get the customer to say "Yes." But many of the messages we give our customers start with "No." No drinks, no pets, no refunds without a receipt, no this, no that... No wonder we don't get enough people saying "Yes!"

In fact, saying "No" to the customer is so common that "No shirt, no shoes, no service" is actually perceived as a clever greeting to customers. Think of it this way: Your customers haven't set foot in your store yet, and you're already telling them, "No."

What's worse are signs that scold the customer, such as "Don't touch." What kind of experience does that provide a customer? When a customer is attracted to something – whether it's a T-shirt, a crystal unicorn, or a ballpoint pen – it's human nature to want to touch it. Touching an item is part of the buying process. *What fabric is this sweater made of? How does this purse strap feel on my shoulder? How does this pen feel in my hand?*

Profitable Retailers replace those "No" signs with "Yes" signs.

Instead of telling customers "No drinks allowed," give them drinks! Yes, a few products will get ruined but it's likely that you'll get more customers in the store, and as a result, sell more products.

I know a store that has a Starbucks next door. Now, most of us would love to have a Profitable Retailer like Starbucks next door. They create an incredible amount of traffic and attract an affluent customer base. What more could you ask for? But this retailer has a "No Drinks" sign on their door! I figure the next sign to go up in the store will be, "Space For Lease."

Replace that "no refunds without a receipt" sign with "refunds gladly made with a receipt." Replace the "no pets" sign with a "pet bar," which could be nothing more than a place outdoors to leave a pet in the shade complete with fresh water. Pet owners will love you, and it will keep the pets outside.

Here are some other examples:

- Replace "No personal checks" with "We accept Visa and MasterCard."

- Take down the "No Admittance" sign to your backroom and replace with "Staff Members Only."

- If you have a "No Cell Phones" sign up, it can be replaced with a "Please Take All Phone Calls Outside."

- If you have "No Shirt, No Shoes, No Service," you have the same sign as a million other retailers. Try being a little more original by putting up a sign that reads "Shirt and Shoes Required."

- Remove the "No Soliciting" sign altogether. You can

always tell a salesperson nicely that you're too busy to meet with him but from time to time you might actually want to learn about something he's selling.

Few stores have merchandise so fragile that customers can't touch it. Sure, an item will be broken from time to time, but that's a cost of doing business. Adopt the policy of a retailer such as Barnes & Noble that has one sample copy of an expensive coffee table book clearly labeled "Sample," while the rest are shrink-wrapped. Every Barnes & Noble sacrifices one book for customers to examine while the rest remain pristine. Both the retailer and the customer benefit.

Signs should be helpful to customers, pointing out departments, sales, new products, and special prices. Signs can be there to inform customers even when a salesperson isn't with them. Signage must always be sensitive to customers. Signs should say "YES!"

The Question: What negative signs in your store can you replace with positive ones?

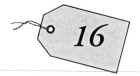

Promises, Promises...

The old saying is true: actions speak louder than words. Profitable Retailers always put the customer first. First before the tasks associated with operating the business. First before profits. (Although putting the customer first will create profits.) First in everything the company does.

As a Profitable Retailer, it's easy to make a promise that you'll get back to a customer about a particular matter. What's harder, though, is to actually do the follow up you've promised. You know how irritating it is when you're waiting for a callback with information. Oftentimes, you can't move forward until you have the information or data you've been promised.

If you need to get back to a customer, don't say something general like "I'll call you later with those numbers." That could mean anything from the next ten minutes until the end of the week. Instead, say, "I expect to have the information by 5 o'clock tomorrow," so the person has some idea of how long to wait before calling back. Be realistic about it, and explain dependencies such as, "I'll have the item tomorrow morning if the UPS™ delivery comes at the usual time."

If the customer waiting to hear from you won't do so for a day or more, call him or her sometime in between just to touch base. Don't assume – wrongly – that the person waiting for you will just presume you don't have the information yet. Let the person know how much longer the wait may be.

If you end up calling back later than you expected, or if the customer ends up calling you first, apologize! But don't go through the excuses, however reasonable they may be. No one is really interested in how busy you are. In fact, giving an excuse can be insulting. When you say, "I'm just so busy," it implies that the other person isn't. Remember that other people are just as busy as you, with as many obligations, emails, and phone calls as you.

If you can't personally get back to the customer, a Profitable Retailer will arrange for someone else to make the call, starting the conversation with "Amy wasn't going to be able to get to you today, so she asked me to call and let you know the status of your order." Being out of the store that day or on vacation is not a valid reason for not making a call you've promised.

Think about what it means to be waiting. Do a quick check each morning. Start your day with the thought, "Is anybody waiting for my call or for me to do something?" If you're aware of other people's time, that caring will come through when you talk to them.

If a customer sounds annoyed, it's because waiting can be a very frustrating experience. This is especially true if the person has adjusted plans to be available at a certain time for your phone call. If a customer keeps her cell phone on all day during a meeting, waiting for a call that doesn't come, she'll finish the day annoyed – with you.

The Question: Do you keep your promises to follow up with customers?

Never Miss Your Second Chance to WOW the Customer

Not long ago, my children and I were in our town center running some errands. One of our stops was a local shoe store. When we arrived at the shoe store, I began looking around and chatting with a salesman about the Red Sox.

I looked over to see my youngest spinning a large sock fixture. Being a retailer, I quickly asked her to stop. I returned to browsing the shoes, oblivious to the fact that my oldest daughter thought she should take the sock fixture for a spin just like her sister. All of a sudden I heard another salesman start yelling in a fairly stern voice, "No. No. No. No. No." I looked over and saw the sock fixture spinning with my daughter standing next to it. He went on to tell her that if she continued to spin the socks, she would have to stay late and pick them up. He clearly was trying to joke with her, but his stern voice had, just as clearly, startled her.

I went back to my shoe browsing, but I was becoming more and more annoyed with what had happened. As a retailer, I don't like parents who let their children run amuck in stores. Without a doubt, if I had known she was spinning the fixture, I would have stopped her. I wasn't bothered by the fact that the salesman told my daughter to stop, but it was his tone and demeanor that bothered me and visibly bothered my daughter.

So here I was standing in the middle of this shoe store with a battle waging in my head between the retailer and the parent. I finally told the salesman we were leaving and would return when his colleague learned to talk to children appropriately.

We left the store and the girls asked if they could play in the park for a few minutes before we headed home. Sitting on a park bench watching them practice their cartwheels, I became more and more annoyed at what had just taken place in the store. I was now mad enough to swear I wouldn't shop in the store again, but, frankly, I wanted to continue to support them.

One thing Profitable Retailers should bear in mind: Most of *your* customers couldn't care less about continued support and would probably just never return. I thought that if I took the time to tell them how unhappy I was, all would be right and I could continue to shop there. The following is a pretty accurate report of the call.

Them: Hello, [name removed] Shoe Store.

Me: Hi. May I speak to the owner or the manager please?

Them: What do you need? *(This isn't starting off well.)*

Me: Is this the owner or manager?

Them: How can I help you? *(For Pete's sake, just answer my question.)*

Me: I'd like to tell you that I was just in the store and am unhappy about how one of your employees talked to my daughter.

Them: Okay. *(He's showing real interest, isn't he?)*

Me: He raised his voice and it clearly shook her up. She shouldn't have been spinning the socks, but he really shouldn't talk to children that way.

Them: Well, I'm sorry. *(Now we're getting somewhere. And then came the word a retailer should never use when a customer is giving you a chance to recover.)* But... *(There it is, the dreaded "but" word.)* ...they don't always hear us and stop.

Me: That still doesn't make it right to use that tone of voice.

Them: You're right; I'm sorry, but... *(There it is again. At this point I don't know what's making me madder, his lack of sincerity or the fact that as a retailer he is totally screwing up this recovery opportunity.)* ...we have problems with children wrecking the store. *(Mind you, this is a family shoe store. It's hardly a business aiming only at an adult customer.)*

Me: *(Now I'm about to lose it.)* You're missing the point. I'm unhappy about your employee and the problem is not what my kid did. I didn't know she was doing it.

Them: I'm sorry. *(I waited and, lo and behold, there was no "but.")* I appreciate you bringing it to my attention. *(He's on a roll.)* And I hope when you come back it doesn't happen again. *(I couldn't believe my ears. That may be the dumbest thing I've ever heard. Is he hoping his salesman doesn't yell at my kid again, or is he hoping my kid doesn't spin the socks again? At this point I'm hoping the guy actually isn't the owner or manager and he lied about that.)*

Me: Whatever. Goodbye.

Them: Thanks again.

There you have it. A wonderful recovery opportunity blown.

Most of the time when we've disappointed our customers, they don't bother to tell us so. *They just leave and become someone else's customer.* When a customer complains to you, he's giving you an opportunity to keep him as a customer. We need to see it as just that – an opportunity. Apologize. Give your customers an incentive to come back into the store again. Thank them for the feedback. Offer to make it right. Do what you have to do, but please, please do not add any "buts."

"Buts" totally invalidate your apology. Just make it right. Don't justify your side. Profitable Retailers stay focused on keeping that person as a customer. If you don't want him as a customer, tell him that and then move on. *But* don't apologize and then invalidate the apology. When you do that, the situation becomes that much worse and that's when he tells his friends, his family, and – if he has a daily newsletter – his readers, all about his negative experience. For me, I think the one thing worse than having to apologize and make it right, is not apologizing and having one less customer.

The Question: Do you keep your "buts" to yourself?

I'm Sorry. Now Spend More Money.

Isn't it interesting how your perspective changes when you're the unhappy customer?

We've all been consumers who have experienced either a business or a product that has failed to meet our expectations and we just want someone to make it right. We're unhappy and we want a solution we believe is fair and reasonable. Unfortunately, now and then we seem to encounter unresponsive and/or uncaring employees who have evidently made it their life mission to make our lives more difficult. And we think to ourselves, "If only someone would listen!"

Right there in that desire to be heard is the key to your happiness as a customer and your success as a retailer. When customers stop doing business with a company, it's frequently not because they didn't like what they heard. Often it's because they don't think anybody's even listening to them. Most unhappy customers are reasonable once they feel that the company representative they're talking to understands the problem and is interested in finding a solution that works for both parties. When you're working with an unhappy customer, it's important to let her vent her frustrations and tell her story.

Once that happens, you can take the lead and transition to the solution.

The secret to the transition, and to making an unhappy customer happy, is really quite simple. After hearing the customer's story, Profitable Retailers take a moment to acknowledge her feelings. This not only lets the customer know you've heard what she's said, but also tells her that you empathize. This acknowledgement does wonders for taking the emotions out of the situation. It strengthens the relationship between the customer and the company because the customer knows that someone understands the issue. Knowing this, the customer is ready to move on to a solution.

Some examples of how to empathize with the customer include:

"That must have been incredibly frustrating."

"I can sure understand why you're so unhappy."

"I would be frustrated, too."

Then follow the acknowledgement with a transition statement:

"Well, let's see what we can do to make it better."

"I'm sure we can fix this together."

Two key points:

- Retailers often confuse acknowledging feelings with admitting wrong. We're acknowledging how the customer feels, not that anyone is wrong. This isn't about apportioning blame.

- Try to use the word "we" rather than "I." It acknowledges to the customer that he or she is an active participant in the solution.

This method of acknowledging the customer's feelings and transitioning to the solution is a surefire way to turn an unhappy customer into a raving advocate.

Some things to think about:

- Your customer doesn't care what you've paid for your merchandise.

- Your customer doesn't care what your costs are.

- Your customer doesn't care how hard it is to find good people.

- Your customer doesn't care what your vendors do or don't do for you.

- Your customer doesn't care that Wal-Mart (or any other store) might pay less than you for the same merchandise.

- Your customer doesn't care how many hours you work.

But!

- Your customer *does* care how much he or she pays for a product.

- Your customer *does* care how that product will benefit him or her.

- Your customer *does* care how much you and your staff know about what you sell.

- Your customer *does* care how neat and clean your store is.

- Your customer *does* care how she or he feels in your store.

- Your customer *does care about how much you care.*

Remember: Customers don't know how much you care until you show them. Respect what is important to them, deliver products, services, and experiences that meet their needs, and you'll have customers who care about you as much as you care about them. And that's how long-term relationships develop and flourish. And that's what will make you successful.

The Question: Are you and your staff practiced in turning unhappy customers into advocates for your store?

Yes, I'd Be Happy to Take That Return

Your return and exchange policy can be a strategic competitive advantage that differentiates you from your competition.

Casual clothing retailer, Lands' End, does just that. Their "Guaranteed. Period." policy has always been an unconditional one that reads: "If you're not completely satisfied with any item you buy from us, at any time during your use of it, return it and we will refund your full purchase price."

Lands' End leverages that policy in their stores, website, and catalog channels. The result is a very dedicated long-term customer base. If a retailer is going to have a liberal return policy, it's a mistake to not use it to his or her advantage. If a liberal policy doesn't result in either more towline or more satisfied customers, it's probably costing the retailer profits.

Another choice is to have a policy that matches your competition. While it won't differentiate your store, it won't disappoint your customer base either. Rarely, if ever, should a retailer ever have a policy that falls short of the competition's policy. Only those retailers who offer a considerable price advantage can get away with offering a limited return and exchange policy, and even those retailers will still find themselves disappointing customers.

Balancing sales, profits, customer expectations, vendor policies, and employee satisfaction is never easy. It's safe to say that the more liberal your return and exchange policy can be, the happier your customers and employees are. The dangerous flipside: Follow too liberal a policy and you'll see your profits dwindle away. Striking the balance is never easy, but then again, no one ever said retailing was easy. If it were, it wouldn't be as profitable.

Don't forget to include your employees when creating your policies. Employees are the most frequently overlooked aspect when considering the impact of a retailer's return and exchange policy. Employees bear the brunt of a customer's displeasure with either the policy itself or the way the policy has been communicated.

Conversely, if the retailer has a liberal return policy, the employees will also benefit. Making sure the employees have good guidelines for applying the policy is important. Creating a decision-making guide can help employees understand what they can and can't do.

Empower your staff to represent your store. Give your employees clear guidance and directions on how to communicate and enforce return guidelines with customers. Don't just preach it – teach it. Use situational role-playing exercises to train them in your policies.

Criticizing your employees' decisions after the fact without offering any guidelines can negatively impact their morale. If employees are not applying the guidelines and policies that have been put into place, then it's important to coach them on how to do so.

Undermining them, especially in front of the customer, is inexcusable. For Profitable Retailers, success comes from not only educating their customers but their employees, as well.

One of the hardest things to teach employees is to not take it personally when a customer is upset about the return and exchange policy. Because of the pride and loyalty they have to you, their employer, employees often personalize what's taking place. It's important that they understand that returns and exchanges come with being a retailer and their goal is to balance the customer's expectations and the store's policies.

The Question: Is it time to re-evaluate your returns and exchange policy to make the policy more effective for your particular store?

To Be Right or to Be Profitable

Obviously the best way to win and keep customers is to give them a great experience every time they walk into your store. But we're all human and from time to time something goes wrong. The customer ends up unhappy.

One Profitable Retailer recently asked my advice about an unhappy customer who wanted a refund. My recommendation was that she refund the woman. My reasoning is that, first of all, you don't want unhappy people to make your life miserable. Giving her the refund makes her happy, which makes you happy. Second, it doesn't matter who is right or wrong; the customer is going to say negative things about you. Not only will you never do business with her again, you also risk losing her friends and family. Over a couple of years it could add up to five to ten times the refund amount.

Another Profitable Retailer had a similar incident and not only refunded the customer's money, but gave her the product as well. Here was a customer who was angry and probably planning to never ever do business with that store again. When he later ran into her, the previously unhappy customer started telling her friend the story and "how great" the retailer was. *Now that's how to be a Profitable Retailer!*

A few things to think about when you run into difficult customers:

Do you want to be right or do you want to be profitable? What's the real cost of losing this customer? What is his or her lifetime value? How would you feel if you were in the customer's shoes?

Don't consider the customer "mean," think of him or her as "unhappy." You can't make a mean customer nice but you can make an unhappy customer into a happy shopper. The difference? At least the power is back in your hands.

No matter what, you don't have to accept unacceptable behavior! What's unacceptable: cursing, yelling, screaming, bullying, pointing, poking, pushing, hitting – basically any kind of behavior that doesn't befit an adult.

Don't forget to help your employees learn techniques for interacting with unhappy customers. Model this behavior for them. When they see that you're happy about resolving an issue so that the customer leaves happy, your employees will do the same. During a slow time, you may want to practice some role-playing exercises so that your employees become confident about their ability to react appropriately with an unpleasant customer.

The Question: When it comes to difficult customers, do you want to be right or do you want to be profitable?

How to Fire an Unprofitable Customer

You know all the signs: the Unprofitable Customer is at it again. He's giving your best salesperson a hard time because you don't ever have what he wants in stock. He wants a discount because the box is dented. He *always* wears a medium – there must be something wrong with *this* shirt (as he pulls at it and sweats in it).

You're gouging him. You're ignoring him. You don't appreciate his business. This is the same customer who demanded an exchange – past your deadline – and you eventually caved in and did the return, despite your best judgment. You've actually wondered why he keeps coming back if he believes your store is this bad.

He's returned used merchandise, complained about almost everything, and no matter what you or your staff have tried, nothing works to make this customer happy.

Most retail stores have one: he's the customer who is impossible to please, although, Lord knows, you've tried. He's the customer who's never happy, thinks you're determined to rip him off, and is sure there's a better deal, a better price, and better service at your competitor.

Don't think this happens to just small stores, however. Awhile back, Filene's Basement in Boston banned two sisters from shopping in all of their twenty-one stores, based on their having repeatedly abused return policies. The incident made national news. While some people may say that all publicity is good, not much good could come out of this publicity.

There may come a time that you may have to do the same thing as Filene's Basement and give the Unprofitable Customer the boot. While it will rarely happen, there does come a time when real life disproves the saying, "The customer is always right."

But how do you do it politely and without making the national news? Because it happens so rarely, most retailers – even Profitable Retailers – don't know how to fire a customer, so they don't. In fact, there are two different ways this can be done.

The first way is the *in-person* firing. It's important to bring closure to the relationship with the customer. Here's how to go about it: Explain to the customer that while you appreciate that he keeps giving you multiple opportunities, it's clear that the store keeps falling short of expectations. That's why it would be in both of your best interests that this be the last time you do business together.

See how easy that is? And how calm?

Then you continue. Explain that it's important that any refunds, exchanges, and purchases happen at this moment because this will be the final time and you will no longer be accepting any transactions with the customer. I think it's very important that the customer be given the last chance. It's also the best chance to end the relationship on a positive note, if that's possible.

The second way to fire a customer is *via the mail or email* with the same exact message. It's important to show that ending the relationship will benefit both parties, and it's not a letter that says you're tired of being treated like a doormat.

Clearly, firing a customer is an action of last resort. It's not a decision to be made lightly. And it's a decision that goes way past the occasional annoying customer or customer who is having a bad day. A "fire-able" customer is one who has materially disrupted your business, disrespected your policies, abused your customer reward programs, and demoralized your staff. Any profit you may have made with this customer's purchases were long ago eaten up with staff time trying to do the impossible – trying to make things right.

One of your best tools in determining whether to fire a customer is to keep accurate sales records for each customer. A POS system, when used properly, is the easiest way to do this. When you know how much a customer's *lifetime value* is to you, you will be able to make the determination more clearly about when (or if) to pull the plug.

Firing a customer is not a decision to make in anger, but only after a thoughtful analysis of the situation is complete. It's not an emotional decision – it's a business decision. When that time comes, remain calm and keep your emotions in check.

The Question: When is a customer's business no longer worth it?

Selling 101 – It Works

Everyone has heard – and probably used – the phrase "features and benefits." Those words have become shorthand for "all the information about the product and what it does." Do your sales associates understand the difference between a feature and a benefit? *Do you?* A thorough understanding of features and benefits – and how they work together – will enable you to sell more products and sell them more effectively.

Let's start off really basic and define those two terms first. A *feature* is something about a product that makes it special or different from similar products. Features include obvious things like size or color, what it's made of, how much it weighs, and even the price.

For example: A two-liter plastic bottle of root beer is different from a twelve-ounce aluminum can of the same root beer. In this example, "two-liter" and "plastic bottle" are features of that particular soda product while "twelve-ounce" and "aluminum can" are features of the second soda product.

Other product features may include dimensions, finish, style, model, season or year, function, or brand. Features of a product distinguish it from a competitor's product or from another model by the same manufacturer. For example, one company may make different washing machines, all of which have different (or slightly different) product features.

A good salesperson knows all the features of a particular product. Customers ask specific questions all the time about a product's features, such as:

- *"What other colors does this purse come in?"*

- *"How much does this watch cost?"*

- *"What is this suit made of?"*

- *"Does this shirt come in extra-large?"*

- *"Is this travel guidebook current?"*

- *"Is this the latest DVD player this company makes?"*

It's clear that having ready answers to these questions can keep the sales process moving forward. Having ready answers also positions your sales associates as product specialists.

Okay, we know what a feature is – so what's a *benefit*? A benefit is slightly more complex because a benefit is in the eye of the beholder – or in this case, in the eye of the buyer. Even the most amazing features – "comes in twenty-three colors!" or "weighs just twelve ounces!" – mean nothing if the buyer doesn't see the benefit in it.

A benefit is the buyer's understanding of "what's in it for me." In the root beer bottle example above, the features are "two-liter" and "plastic bottle," but the benefits are "can serve your whole family" or "plastic bottle won't break" or "can screw top back on bottle to save root beer for later." To further the analysis, the feature of the two-liter root beer is a price of $1.39, but the benefit is "saves money over buying root beer in cans."

A particular aspect of a product can be both a feature and a benefit. A day-glo orange (feature) suitcase can stand out in a crowd of black suitcases in baggage claim (benefit). In this case, the feature or color of the suitcase is obvious to the customer, but the benefit might not be.

Customers talk a lot about features since they use features to compare different products. Features are easy to see with their own two eyes. The briefcase has a side pocket. The price is $9.99. The dress is made from velvet. The pitcher holds thirty-two ounces. Customers don't buy on features, though. They buy based on the *perceived* benefit associated with the product.

Always "translate" a feature into a benefit. A customer may know the particular price for a piece of electronics. You can say, "These prices have come down tremendously in the past few months. This particular product used to sell for $300 more, so you're really getting a great value."

Here's another example: A customer sees a brand name. That's just a feature. You need to add: "This company is by far the leader in the field and has been the leader in developing the new technology, so whatever you buy from them will be the best quality." Having your staff understand – and be able to articulate – both features and benefits will make the sales process easier. For example, questions often arise about price. *Why does one set of sheets cost more than another set of sheets?* That's a common question. Then you can say, "These sheets have a 600-thread count (feature), so it makes the material incredibly soft (benefit)."

Call it the power of "so" – the bridge between a feature and a benefit.

Some other examples include:

- "This radio is waterproof, *so you can use it in the shower.*"

- "This blender has ten speeds, *so you can use it to chop and blend and everything in-between.*"

- "This scarf has this bold pattern with about six different colors, *so it can be worn with just about anything in your closet.*"

- "This cordless phone has the ability for the base to buzz the handset, *so if you lose the handset in your home, you can easily find it.*"

At your next staff meeting, grab five items off your sales floor and have your staff see if they can describe the features and the benefits of each using this exercise above. Remember that all customers don't know what you know, so even the most apparent benefit may not be so apparent to some of your customers. That's why all salespeople should be selling features and benefits in partnership.

The Question: Are you and your sales associates talking about features and benefits?

Expect a Lot, Receive a Lot

I often talk with retail executives from around the country who are unhappy with the level of customer service or experience their company is providing. Their stores are not necessarily giving poor customer experiences, but they are falling short of their own company's expectation.

When this happens, the executives almost always seem to question the effectiveness of their training and want to "fix the training problem." What they don't realize is that most customer experience doesn't fall short because of ineffective training. The root of the problem is frequently the failure of managers to set and maintain the appropriate expectations.

To set expectations, the owners or managers need to determine what needs to take place in the store. Is every customer welcomed? Is there a sales process to be used? Is there a customer service standard? What processes are to be done on a regular basis?

Expectations must also be clearly communicated to the staff, unless you've hired mindreaders. Employees need to understand what the expectations are for them and the reward or consequence for meeting or not meeting them.

Most retailers fall short in their customer experience approach because local and area management don't demand that standards be met. When I was stranded in Columbus, Ohio, one weekend, I stayed at two different Marriott hotels. While I believe that employees at both hotels had gone through similar training, the difference between the two was like night and day. In one hotel, when I said "thank you," I got the all too familiar "no problem" in response.

In the other hotel when I said "thank you," the employee responded with, "It was my pleasure." At one Marriott they used my name each time they interacted with me. Nobody at the other one ever addressed me by name. Same chain, same town, different results. I can't help but believe that the difference was the hotel managers and the expectations they set for their employees.

Expectations of how the customer should be engaged and treated must be articulated, documented, measured, and then required by senior management. It starts at the very highest levels of an organization and must then be transferred from one level of management to the next.

Any level of management that falls short in setting an expectation of their employees will break the chain, and the customer will not receive the expected experience. I'm often amazed by how high up the chain breaks in some organizations. I've declined consulting jobs because I knew that senior management was not committed to the customer experience. They said one thing, but their actions demonstrated something else.

A company must have appropriate training programs and resources, but the best programs are only as effective as the expectations for the learned skills and behavior.

One of the reasons I admire and respect the retailer, Build-A-Bear Workshop®, is because of the incredibly consistent experience they deliver throughout their stores. That happens because every executive, every field manager, and every store manager at Build-A-Bear is committed to delivering the experience that's been defined and expected by the organization.

Many retailers who had great products, great location, and a good strategy have failed because of poor execution. More often than not, poor execution isn't because staff skills are lacking, but because each level of the organization fails to hold the next one accountable. Profitable Retailers find that a good strategy with the appropriate training and the right expectation will most certainly find success.

The Question: Are you and your team setting the right expectations and holding employees accountable?

Employee Relations

Your competitors can sell what you sell and even sell it for less. Your competitors can copy your store and merchandising too. What they can't do is copy your people. Doesn't it make sense to ensure that they are trained, happy, and knowledgeable about the products they sell? The days of the big, bad boss are gone. Profitable Retailers are three parts coach, two parts colleague, and one part boss.

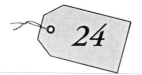

My Best Management Lesson

Every Christmas I'm reminded of one of the best management lessons I ever learned. It was 1989 and I was an assistant manager at The Sharper Image in Palm Beach Gardens, Florida. On the Sunday before Christmas we were mobbed from open to close; it was a record-breaking day.

Actually, the day had been a lot of fun, and the entire staff was in a good mood. All day the store manager, Keith, talked about the lobster dinner he was going to cook that night after work for some friends who were visiting. Keith, who was from New Orleans, had said to me, "Buddy, it's going to be an exceptional dinner and evening."

At the end of the day, I told him I would close out the register. While going through the closing out process, the system jammed up. Without thinking, I did the unthinkable.

I rebooted.

And to my utter disbelief and considerable horror, when the system booted up, every single sale from the day was gone. Every single sale vanished.

All I could think was that Keith was going to kill me.

Knowing how much Keith was looking forward to that lobster dinner, I dreaded the conversation we were about to have. I walked over to where he was feverishly cleaning and reluctantly told him that I had wiped out the entire day's sales, and I would have to re-ring every single one. I quickly added that he could go on home to his dinner, and I would stay by myself and ring them.

He looked at me with a smile and said, "Buddy, things happen. The lobster can wait. Let's get busy."

About four hours later, well past the dinner hour, we finished the last transaction, and I closed out the register correctly. As we were leaving, I asked how he could be so calm about what happened. He looked at me and said, "An employee's first mistake is always on me. Make the same mistake twice, and I won't be so understanding. Time for me to go home and have some lobster. Merry Christmas, Doug."

I replied, "Merry Christmas, Keith. Thank you for being so understanding."

As I watched Keith walk down the mall hallway, he turned, looked back at me, and yelled, "No problem, buddy, the first mistake is always on me." He turned the corner and headed home to his much-anticipated lobster dinner.

The management lesson I learned from Keith that night is one of the best presents I've ever received. It's one I gladly pass on to other Profitable Retailers. *By claiming the first mistake for the employee, you allow the employee to grow and learn from his or her mistake.*

We can't learn from our mistakes if we're worried about how much trouble we're in when we make the mistake. People will almost invariably cause more damage covering up their mistakes than by the mistakes themselves. And, besides, for the most part, employees don't make mistakes on purpose. I knew how to close out the register correctly but, that one time, I messed it up. On purpose? Of course not.

So the next time an employee makes a major mistake that causes your blood to boil, don't yell. Count to ten and repeat these words in a soothing voice: "Don't worry. Things happen. The first mistake is always on me."

Believe me, after hearing those words from Keith, I never ever made a mistake closing out the register again. I also became a better manager because of them.

Every Christmas, I think of Keith and the management lesson he taught me, and for that I am grateful. And wherever he is, I hope he is happy and still enjoying a lobster dinner.

The Question: Are your employees willing to admit to you that they've made a mistake?

Scheduling People to Please and Profit

There are times on all business calendars when it's necessary to require people to work when they would rather not. Some employees don't want to work on the weekends or evenings, but you may need more coverage during those times. But how do you do that? How do you develop schedules that are fair and effective and don't leave you worried about providing good service to your customers? My advice:

Talk to employees about your needs as far in advance as possible. Don't wait for the day before you need someone to work to drop the bomb. Rather, discuss the situation as a group, so the team can talk about what coverage is needed, what skills need to be present, and what combinations of people have those skills. If someone is available, that employee might not mind working over Memorial Day weekend or on Super Bowl Sunday.

Always have a back up. If you're not sure how busy you'll be, it might make sense to have an employee on standby ready to come in if needed. It's a safe bet that most of your employees have cell phones, so if you're not sure how busy you're going to be, you may make arrangements to have extra staff on standby. Most people would agree to be available in the local area and be willing to come in on short notice.

Don't overdo it. If you need specific skills on weekends, that's fine, but Profitable Retailers don't make the arbitrary assignment that there must be *X* number of staff on site at all times. Let the staff help you set those criteria.

Consider your normal weekend day of business. It could be that it only makes sense for people to work half-shifts. For example, if you're typically really busy on Saturday mornings, and then dead until closing, you might arrange for an employee to work just one half-day.

Take volunteers first – and offer an incentive for bad-shift coverage. *Ask and you shall receive.* You may be surprised by who volunteers to work during an undesirable time. For example, someone's significant other may have to work weekends, too, so your employee may be just as glad to be at work. It's a fact that many employees with children prefer to work the weekend shift so they can be available for childcare during the week.

Plus, if employees see that this is a team effort and that everyone sacrifices at some point, they may be more likely to volunteer if their schedules allow. Profitable Retailers understand that the incentive for working a bad shift doesn't have to be financial. Giving them alternate or extra time off is usually a good offering.

Finally: Thank the employee who is willing to work on December 26 or Labor Day weekend. If an employee feels as if he or she is extending him- or herself or doing you a favor, you can at least acknowledge it. Most of the time, a sincere thank you in front of his or her peers will go a long way to show your appreciation. And it will set a precedent and expectation other employees will want to live up to.

The Question: Do your employees have a say in shift scheduling?

I Can't. I Won't. *You Will.*

On more than one occasion, a client has asked me what to do about employees who refuse to do something asked of them. It can be quite frustrating to deal with, especially when it's an employee who might excel in other areas. So I always share with my clients one of the best and simplest coaching/people management lessons I was ever taught.

When an employee isn't doing something you've asked him to do, you need to determine if the employee is saying through his actions, "I can't do it" or "I won't do it." In other words, does the problem stem from the employee's attitude, or is it a sign that he needs something else from you in order to do the job?

This is a very important first step, because some employees have a hard time admitting they can't perform a task, so their natural fallback position may be to not do it at all. It doesn't mean they're lazy or they should be fired – it just means that they don't have all the knowledge and information they need to perform the job to your expectations. Here are a few tips to use when you assess the issue:

Question the issue. Always assume employees mean "I can't" when you first address the issue. Then sit down and ask questions to determine how you can help them move to "I can."

- *Do your employees need training and skill development?*
  Maybe you can role-play with them. Many tasks
  you perform are second nature to you, but can be
  intimidating to an employee, such as setting the alarm or
  preparing a bank deposit. You might want an employee
  to greet each customer, but the employee may be shy or
  stumped as to what to say beyond a meek, "Hi." Here's
  a case where actually providing your employee with a
  scripted greeting might work wonders. You can make a
  game out of role-playing. After the employee has role-
  played greeting you half a dozen times, he or she will
  feel more comfortable doing it with actual customers.

- *Do they need more direction?* Maybe you can show them
  again what your expectation is. Organizations work best
  when there are systems in place. It may make you crazy
  to hear the phone going unanswered. That's why it's a
  good idea to say, "The phone must be answered within
  three rings. If you're with a customer, here's a good way
  to break away to answer the phone..." and then give
  them an example. Some of what you tell employees may
  seem too obvious to mention, but you can never go
  wrong articulating the obvious. Instead of saying, "You
  can take a break now," you might want to say, "You can
  take a 15-minute break now and be back at the register
  at 3:20." A chronically late employee truly might not
  realize how important it is to be back to work on time.

- *Do they simply need help?* Maybe you can give them
  some tools or some hands-on assistance. Managers have
  to strike a balance between supervision and delegation.
  You may think you're "hovering," but there are some
  employees who welcome your supervision. You might

say, "Let's walk through what happens when a customer wants to buy a gift card" or "Let me show you some tricks I've learned about folding shirts." When you approach your employee as a coach who wants to improve performance, your input will be appreciated.

Whatever it is that's causing employees to say, "I can't," you need to identify it. Then you need to give them the tools, training, and assistance that will move them to "I can." Afterwards, you and your employees can agree from now on that "they will."

Be direct. If the employee is still not doing what's being asked, it's a case of "I won't," which needs to be addressed directly and simply by saying, "Either you will, or I won't continue to employ you."

Get real. What if the employees say "I can," when in actuality they "can't," and the job you asked them to do comes out like a disaster even after you've worked hard to train them? That's when you need to determine if they can ever do what's being asked.

The fact is from time-to-time people end up in the wrong job. Nobody wants to fail, but if they can't do the job, they can't do the job. And the company is failing the employee if they let an employee stay in a job that just doesn't fit.

But if you followed the first step, they can never say you didn't try to help.

So the next time you encounter this issue, whether at the store or at home (since this even works with kids), ask yourself if it's a case of "I can't" or "I won't." And remember, the first time you address an issue, always assume it's an "I can't." Our role as

Profitable Retailers is to help our employees be successful, so our stores can be successful.

The Question: When you have an employee issue you've put off dealing with, are *you* saying you "can't" or "won't"? (I'm saying *you can.*)

Coach, Your Team Needs Feedback

When speaking with an employee about behavior that needs to change, how you speak to the employee will affect the outcome. Choosing the right words and the right tone just might be enough to turn an employee around. Of course, any discussion with an employee should be private – out of earshot and visual range of other employees.

"Praise in public; coach in private" is a good slogan for managers. If you're telling an employee that she has done a great job, say it in front of her peers. It multiplies the power of your comments.

However, in any discussion with an employee that's corrective in nature, Profitable Retailers begin with a positive comment and end with a positive comment. You might have to calm down a bit to be able to be that rational about your talk, but it's a better way to go.*

---

* Horror stories abound about employees getting fired on Christmas Eve or reprimanded on their birthday or right after a tragedy has happened in the employee's life. Before you launch into why and how the employee needs to change, you may want to make sure that he or she hasn't recently experienced an incident that may have negatively impacted his or her life.

Think of yourself as a coach. A coach is a person who understands strategy, sees the big picture of the game, and wants the team to win. When you watch a professional coach, you see that he or she doesn't just reprimand the players' behavior. The coach tells players what needs to be done to turn the game around. Frame your comments as if you're a helpful coach. Your goal is to show your employees ways to improve.

Be empathetic. Try to put yourself in the place of your employee. When you do, you may be more able to express sincere concern. You will be able to share with your employee ways to make the work situation better. It's easy to break into a litany of "shoulds." You should have locked the storeroom, because you should know we have had some problems," or "If you had gotten to work on time like you should and brought your nametag like you should…" Dwelling on the incorrect behavior does nothing to change future behavior.

Here's an example. Let's say you have an employee you feel is curt with customers to the point that you've noticed customers are offended. Start the conversation off with a positive comment such as, "I want to talk to you today about some things I've noticed in the store, but first I want to tell you how much I appreciate that I can depend on you to show up on time and go the extra mile no matter what I ask from you."

Then you can segue into the problem to be addressed: "I know the store can get really crazy at times when there are customers asking questions, UPS needs a signature, and the phone is ringing." You might continue, "It's difficult when so much is going on to not let it affect us, but it's part of our job to stay calm – especially when we're talking to customers." Give a specific example such as, "I noticed when that older gentleman this morning asked if we had that new backpack in navy, you said 'nope.' Of course, you answered his question, but there are better ways that sound more caring – and ways that don't take more than a few more seconds – to give." Then explore with your employee different answers he could have given. End on a positive and remind your employee you'll continue to monitor the situation.

Once you have established that the employee's actions were not appropriate, spend your time exploring how future behavior can be changed. Follow up the conversation with a written summary of the agreed-upon changes, and schedule a meeting a few weeks in the future to review the employee's progress.

Profitable Retailers always end the conversation by repeating their confidence in the employee's ability to do what you're asking them to do. Knowing they have the coach's support and confidence may give them the renewed spirit to try to win the game for you.

The Question: Are you a good coach for your team?

Beware of the "In-Betweener"

Filling an open staff position can take much of your time
– running an ad, background checks, scheduling, conducting
interviews, etc. When you finally make a decision to hire
one particular individual, it's time to get back to your normal
routine and other projects in the store that may have been
neglected during the hiring process.

Even with a good orientation for new hires, it's easy to make
excuses for mistakes a new employee makes. It's true – with the
exception of those near-perfect employees (I call them Great
Employees) – new employees make mistakes until they learn
all the practices and procedures as well as the culture of your
particular store.

You may have a policy to put a new employee on probation
for a few weeks or a few months to see if the employee "works
out." There are very good reasons for doing this, not the least
of which is to keep your eye on the employee to evaluate his or
her performance. At the end of the probationary period, you
can make your decision as to whether this person stays on as a
permanent employee.

One of the good business reasons for this is to make sure you haven't hired what one HR guru calls the "in-betweener." This is the employee who is never bad enough to fire – he doesn't come in drunk or steal or snap at customers, but he's always lagging behind and his performance is never quite good enough to satisfy you.

Even Profitable Retailers have gotten stuck with an in-betweener. She's the one who you don't quite trust to telephone a vendor with an order. She's the one that you may keep away from your best customer. But in-betweeners never are quite bad enough to do something about.

When an employee needs to be fired, typically the proof is clear – not showing up for work, physically confronting a co-worker, chronic tardiness, insubordination, etc. But once an in-betweener has settled in, that person is tough to fire. And so that employee drifts year-after-year annoying the heck out of you with barely adequate job performance. How do you fire someone who has worked for you for ten years and has never done anything really worthy of termination?

But it gets worse. As a manager, you will spend an inordinate amount of time supervising this employee. The in-betweener will drain your time and your energy in a way other employees won't and don't. After all, this is the employee that you can never quite trust to do something right, to do something in a timely manner, to do a project thoroughly or to use his best judgment.

Profitable Retailers monitor new employees early on so that they don't get stuck. If you do, employees' poor performances will be your fault. And as an owner of a small retail business, you don't even have the option open to managers in large companies. At least they can transfer the in-betweener to another department – you're stuck.

One possible solution is to devise your own litmus test. After the probationary period for a new hire, ask yourself, "Would I trust this employee to call my best customer?" or "Is this employee capable of closing the store by himself?" or "Would I send this employee to the bank with the weekend receipts?" Every Profitable Retailer will have his or her own litmus test. If it's clear the new employee has not earned your trust (and likely never will), it's best to cut your losses. There are Great Employees out there. Don't settle for the in-betweener.

The Question: What are you doing to make sure you don't get stuck with an in-betweener?

Be a Mentor for Your New Managers

For some of your employees, their position at your store will be the first time they are in a position to manage other people. Even Profitable Retailers will confess that managing people is the most difficult part of their jobs.

Before you promote or hire a person into a position where the employee will be managing people, it's a good idea to explore with that person her experiences and attitudes about motivating and managing. This is a good conversation to have over a casual lunch. Ask your manager-candidate questions such as:

- *"What do you think the best part of being a manager is?"*

- *"What's the hardest part of being a manager?"*

- *"Can you tell me about a time when you think a manager handled a staff situation well?"*

- *"Can you tell me about a time when a manager handled a staff situation not so well?"*

- *"When there's a problem in the store, whose fault is it typically?"*

- *"What are we doing that we should be doing more of? Less of?"*

Becoming a first-time supervisor can be quite a shock for some, when the new manager realizes that being the boss is not always the dream job he or she thought it might be.

Here are some tips to share with new managers:

"Be a communicator." Good communicators pay close attention to the person speaking to them, and provide a clear and thoughtful response. Good communicators give careful instructions and speak with confidence and purpose. Developing communications skills will go a long way in building credibility as a manager.

Another good piece of advice is to learn the benefits of listening. Listening is a skill that can be developed and will serve any manager well.

"Monkey see, monkey doesn't have to do." Make sure your new manager knows that there are many effective styles of management and that you don't expect him to become a "mini-me." You manage one way; your employee may manage in a totally different way. Make sure the new manager understands that changing the basic way you interact with people once you've landed the job is usually unnecessary. The fact is folks rise into management because they've earned the respect and trust of peers and superiors. Their personality is suited for the role, and they are competent at their jobs.

"You'll find out who your friends are." The most difficult part of being promoted to manager is how it can change the relationships with former peers. True friends and mature people can separate their roles at work from their personal relationships; however, a new manager needs to be prepared to make difficult and sometimes unpopular decisions that can strain personal relationships formed in the workplace.

"Change slowly." Some new managers are so anxious to make their marks that they want to throw out the systems, forms, and procedures that were in place and make up new ones with their own personal stamp on them. Rather than encouraging them to "make any changes you want," urge them to take their time to see which parts of the store are working and which aren't. It's better to start out with "business as usual" until the new manager feels confident about changes.

"Take the lead." Although the new manager needs to know that you will be there to answer questions, Profitable Retailers encourage new managers to make their own decisions. The new manager needs to know that he or she has been selected for the position based on the potential for sound judgment. Of course, mistakes will be made, and those mistakes can be viewed as part of the informal orientation process of being a new manager.

The Question: Do you help your new managers to succeed?

Good Managers Start as Good Assistant Managers

This chapter is written specifically for assistant managers and other non-store-manager key carriers. I encourage you to pass it on to them.

Profitable Retailers know that being an assistant manager is by far one of the toughest positions in retail. All of us who have risen through the retail ranks have been in your position. You don't have as much say in policies as you'd like, you're expected to maintain standards, and you have some management duties – but a lot of what you do is the same as the rest of staff. You're a "'tweener," stuck in no-person's land between staff and management. You often feel under-appreciated for what you do, no matter how hard you work. I know, because I've been there.

What I've learned through the years is that the stronger the assistant manager is, the better the store. Here is what I've seen winning assistant managers do that improves the overall store performance as well as prepare them to be successful store managers:

The standards of the store never change, whether the store

manager is on duty or not. When I worked for The Sharper Image, the company dictated what music could and could not be played in the store. I discovered once that my assistant manager bent that rule when she was manager on duty. While it looked like a small thing, and the employees liked listening to their own music, the assistant actually was losing her credibility with the staff. They learned from her that when she was on duty, the rules didn't apply. Over a period of time the customer feedback and mystery shopper reports were lower when she was manager on duty than when she wasn't. After I coached her about why it was important for her to maintain standards to maintain her position, the store improved and the staff had more respect for her. What didn't change was the grumbling about having to go back to the standard music, of course.

Winning assistant managers never have "off the record" conversations with the staff. As an assistant manager you represent the company in every conversation with employees and customers alike. I'm sorry to admit that I didn't always follow this when I was an assistant manager. Often I wanted to show the employee how much I was "in the know" and that yes, I was a mover and shaker. Actually I wasn't a mover and shaker; I was a gossip. Even worse, I was a gossip in a position of power. Successful assistant managers know that what's talked about behind closed doors, stays behind closed doors, and that all conversations are on the record.

Last but not least, the best assistant managers know that being a leader isn't about a title; it's about leading by example. It's about going first. It's about having the drive and passion to be the best at engaging the customer, the best at making sales, and the best at delighting the customer. It's about being the best so others can learn from you, and not about pride and ego. It's about asking others to role-play with you, where you play the associate or rep first and the associate plays the customer. It's about being as good as a student as you are a teacher. It's about being a winning assistant manager and knowing your time will come.

It's not surprising that I have found that the best store managers were terrific assistant managers. They learned to master the "'tweener" position; they learned to lead and most of all, they learned to learn.

The Question: What have you learned today, what have you taught today, and most of all, what have you done to lead by example?

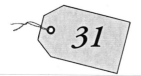

Good? Yes, but You Can Be Better.

Profitable Retailers are good managers, but they always strive to be *great* managers. Here are ten things you can do today (or tomorrow) to be a better store manager:

1. Take one of your employees out for a cup of coffee and spend some quality one-on-one time. Be sure and ask what *you* can do to improve the store and make it a more enjoyable place to work. Also ask what you can do to help them develop.

2. Watch and listen to your staff interact with customers, and then give them feedback. First, tell them three things they did well. Then tell them three things they could have done better. Always end a feedback session expressing your confidence in them and your appreciation for their efforts.

3. Create a fun, one-day contest that involves the whole staff. Here's one that is fun to do and fun to watch: First, pick an area of focus. It could be selling products over a certain price point. Or it could be selling add-ons or complete solutions. One of my favorites is exhibiting a desired behavior you want your employees

to emulate. Purchase a bouquet of flowers and put it into a container in the backroom or on the back counter. Then with either plastic bottles or cups create a vase for each employee working that day. Every time an employee achieves the goal you've set they move a flower from the bouquet into their vase. At the end of the day the employee with the most flowers in their vase wins. The winner gets to take the flowers home as well as something like a gift certificate to a local restaurant.

4. Always, always, always, thank your employees for their contributions and efforts when they're leaving for the day.

5. Spend fifteen minutes working on your own development. Whether it's by reading a book, a magazine, or a newspaper, you must drive your own development. To develop as leaders, we must always be expanding our own base of knowledge.

6. Straighten up your office. You can't expect your employees to have spotless work spaces if you don't.

7. Be the first one to clean in the morning or at closing. It's amazing how much your staff respects you when you join in and clean. I know you have a lot of other things to do, but working side-by-side with your staff is invaluable.

8. One of the biggest mistakes store managers can make is to spend hours working in the office and then come out on to the floor and try to take charge. The best thing you can do when you come onto the floor is to ask the staff how you can help. So often I see a manager come out from the office, see a customer in the store and

ask an employee if they've been helped. You know the employee is dying to tell the manager, "If you'd been on the floor you'd know that we've approached him twice." Come out to help, not take charge.

9.   Engage a customer, and be the reference standard. Successful managers know that there is no such thing as "do as I say and not as I do." If the reference is to welcome every customer then the manager should be out front welcoming every customer. Leaders always go first.

10. Repeat the first nine things every day!

The Question: What have you done today to be a better manager? What will you do tomorrow?

Do You Hear What I Don't Hear?

Clearly communicating your expectations, standards, and agenda to your staff is crucial to a successful operation. Profitable Retailers know that their words and conversations are just one way to communicate. Whether you are aware of it or not, your actions communicate volumes to employees. That's why it's crucial to make sure your actions match your words. Take a look at this conversation:

Me: What's that you say?

Manager: I didn't say anything.

Me: Yes you did.

Manager: No I didn't.

Me: Yes you did. Your actions just spoke loud and clear.

Manager: Really?

Me: Sure. So what have you recently said without saying it?

Manager: Well, I guess when I made fun of that customer after he left the store I was telling the staff that we don't value the customer as much as we say we do.

Me: Oh, really. What else have you told your staff without saying it?

Manager: I guess after I talked about Sara, our new part-timer, to Amy, the other part-timer, I was telling people it's okay to gossip.

Me: Not good, huh?

Manager: Definitely not. I guess telling my staff that I didn't agree with the new sales process corporate says we have to do wasn't the best thing I could have said.

Me: Ouch. What do think you told them by saying that?

Manager: Well, first I told them something I shouldn't have. As a member of management, I need to embrace the new process. Even if I don't necessarily agree with it, I still shouldn't have said so. I realize that I said, without saying it, that there is an "us," the stores, and a "them," the corporate office, instead of acting like we're one company, which we are.

Me: Exactly. You're getting the hang of hearing what you say without saying it.

Manager: Thanks, I think. I know one thing, I'm really sorry I told the staff we could eat and drink on the sales floor unless someone from corporate was visiting.

Me: I'm sure that's one you can easily fix.

Manager: True. But I don't even want to think what I told people when I said it was okay to sign timecards at the start of the week even though we're not supposed to sign them until the end of the week.

Me: What do you think that untold message was?

Manager: Hmm. . . Well, it could mean it's okay to not follow processes. Even more serious, I guess some people could interpret what I said as suggesting that it's okay to fudge paperwork, which is not okay because it's dishonest.

Me: This figuring out what you're saying by actions isn't always fun, is it?

Manager: Not at all.

Me: The cool thing is that you can say a lot by doing positive things as well.

Manager: You mean by executing the customer experience the same way I'm expecting the staff to do?

Me: Exactly. Your actions tell them a lot. Your actions convey your commitment to the experience as well. Your actions also tell your staff that, as a manager, you're not expecting anything of them that you're not expecting of yourself. There are many ways you can give positive messages that are heard, but not said... But I better go, I'm getting up to my maximum word count if I want to call this a medium-length chapter.

Manager: That's cool. By the way, what are you telling me that you're not telling me with this conversation we just had?

Me: Well that's for me not to say and for you to not hear but learn.

Manager: You're strange.

Me: Thanks . . . I heard that.

The Question: When employees observe you, what do your actions tell them that may contradict your words?

Marketing

"If you build it, they will come…"
only works in the movies.
Profitable Retailers know that in
real life, success depends on attracting
and retaining customers through
a variety of marketing techniques.
Profitable Retailers know that
marketing isn't an expense, it's
an investment in their stores.

Marketing: So Much More Than Advertising

A Profitable Retailer once said, "Market like every day is a grand opening and you're short on cash." I love that line. It doesn't mean: "Run an advertisement so you can check off advertising from your to-do list."

Advertising is the act of using a medium to bring public attention to your products and services. *Marketing* is the act of identifying and reaching your customers for the purpose of selling goods and services.

Advertising is an element of marketing, but marketing is so much more than just advertising. First, you must identify your customer. You can't be all things to all people. When you attempt to serve a customer base that's too wide, you become irrelevant to practically everyone. You must intimately know your potential customers.

For example, it would seem very logical to run a store ad in the local newspaper – after all, most people in town read it. Consider though: How many of those readers are your actual customers? Let's say you own a bridal store. There are far more efficient ways to market to potential customers – newly engaged couples, wedding-planners – than a newspaper ad. Don't pay hundreds of dollars to reach people who are not your customers.

In keeping with the bridal shop example, you may better reach customers by using your marketing dollars to exhibit at a bridal fair, host your own fashion show, or rent the names of subscribers in your area from one of the established bridal magazines and use direct mail. This doesn't mean advertising is the wrong approach – the local newspaper may have a yearly bridal section, which would be a great place for your advertisement.

Here's another way to look at it: good marketing is like a cloud of smoke that surrounds your customers. People within the cloud see your ads, read about your store in the local media, and hear about your store from their friends. Another layer of the smoke is the positive experiences people have in your store.

Marketing is all about finding ways to tell people about your store, your products, and your services. The good news is that good marketing doesn't have to break the bank. Some businesspeople equate "good marketing" with how many dollars are spent. Saying "I spent $5,000 on advertising last year" isn't necessarily something to brag about. Consider all the ways you can reach your customer – especially the nontraditional approaches that will cost you very little.

Profitable Retailers know there are ways to market their businesses that don't include buying advertising space or time. You'll find many examples in this book.

The Question: What ideas come to mind for ways to market your store?

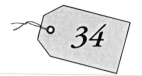

Market Position for the Non-MBA

Market position means having a very clear representation of your store. It's what you sell and how you represent your product through merchandising, marketing, and customer service in relationship to the rest of the market. Profitable Retailers know that if they fail to correctly identify a market position, then their long-term profits and viability are threatened.

Think about the business of selling jeans. Wal-Mart, Target, Gap®, J.C. Penney®, T.J. Maxx®, and Saks Fifth Avenue are just a few of the retailers that sell jeans. Local boutiques, regional chains, flea markets, and a host of other stores are also in the jean business. What are the different market positions of these retailers? That can be determined by the fashion, service, price, and selection offered by each. Profitable Retailers define their own market position as well as those of their key competitors.

This sounds more complicated than it is.

Here's an example outside of retail: Domino's Pizza® is a very successful enterprise that promises its customers pizza delivery in thirty minutes. Few people would argue that Domino's Pizza is the best pizza they've ever eaten. And yet, the enterprise thrives. That's because Domino's knows its market position is supplying pizza for people who are in a hurry and don't want to wait a long time.

There's not one "right" market position. Think about the crucial elements of retail: service, selection, location, price, or quality, and then consider which two of these are your strongest points. A gift shop in a hotel lobby is usually limited by space, so it can't compete on selection. However, this store wins hands-down on location and price. We've all no doubt paid exorbitant amounts of money for aspirin in a hotel gift shop because we're not price sensitive – same with food concessions at airports. You wouldn't pay $7 for a bagel and orange juice anywhere but an airport.

Profitable Retailers pick a market position from the best opportunity based upon the current competition and customer base. Let's imagine you own a florist shop next door to a hospital. Your market position would include, of course, location, but it might also include service. Being so close to the hospital, you can deliver your arrangements quickly, even within the hour.

Here's another example: Many discount clothing stores have "open" dressing rooms, where people are in one big room trying on clothes, rather than in individual, private cubicles. If you're paying $50 for a $300 dress at a discounter, you don't mind the lack of privacy – in fact, you expect it. But if you're paying $300 for a $300 dress, you expect a private cubicle and a salesperson on call for you.

When it comes to quality, consider owning a store that sells wallets. Your customer can buy a wallet for a few dollars or a few thousand dollars. Your market position might include quality – you don't sell inexpensive wallets with Velcro closings; you sell top-quality leather pieces instead. There's nothing wrong with a wallet on either end of the spectrum – just know your place on the spectrum and stick to it.

The Question: What are the two elements that are the foundation of your market position?

Be More Than a Store. Be a Brand.

Profitable Retailers know that successful stores have personality, which is another way of saying successful stores have brands. Brands are not just for huge companies – your store needs a brand, too. So much more than a logo, your store's brand character defines every aspect of your operation.

Pick up any book on marketing or any business magazine, and one word is likely to pop out: branding. Maybe you've been told that you have to "brand" your store or "do a good job of branding." Much confusion exists about what a brand is and what branding means for your store.

Simply stated, a brand is the feelings, opinions, and visions you have for your store that are translated into an experience consistently provided for your customers. Your brand character is a definition of what you want your store to be and what you want your store to stand for. Your brand character is what you want your customers to experience each and every time they are in your store.

What store does a good job at branding? Williams-Sonoma for one. When you go into their store, you see the entire Williams-

Sonoma lifestyle displayed. There are food samples, cooking demonstrations, and displays of Williams-Sonoma products in use.

If someone blindfolded you and walked you into a Williams-Sonoma store, after taking the blindfold off once you were inside, you would probably be able to guess what store you walked into. Most people, without even seeing the Williams-Sonoma sign outside or the name on the products, would recognize the look and ambience of the store. If you can guess what store you're in without seeing any signage, that store has a strong brand.

In their own stores, Profitable Retailers communicate this brand experience to their customers through the senses: how you answer the phone, the look of your front door, how your store smells, how your sales associates look, the cleanliness of your store, whether you have music playing, how merchandise is displayed – *everything*.

"Neighborhood bicycle store" is not a brand. Neither is "huge consumer electronics store." Those descriptions are positions, though the positioning of your store may include parts of your brand character. For example, being a neighborhood store may be part of your brand character, but the brand character is so much more than this one element. Positioning can be described in one sentence: "Bill's Bikes is a store that caters to families buying bikes for their children."

Describing your store's brand character takes more time and more words. Phil Glowatz is a partner in JPGroupUSA, a firm that works with companies to establish and maintain their brand identities. He says, "A brand can't be expressed in one sentence. An analogy is how you'd describe a person. You can't describe everything about a person in one sentence. A person has a richness that you learn about over time."*

When you create a brand, you're creating an emotional experience for your customers. The quick and common definition: "A brand is a promise." You're promising your customers that they will have a consistent experience each time they shop with you.

The Question: What are the components of your store's brand?

---

* Interview with Phil Glowatz. March 15, 2005.

Creative Briefs
(Not the Kind You Wear)

When big advertising agencies meet with their clients for a particular project, the agency personnel receive input about the direction and scope of the project and then take that input and craft what is called a "creative brief." Let's take the example of a shoe store that wants to produce an ad about buying back-to-school shoes. The agency and store people will discuss what is expected from this ad. What is its message? Who should see the ad? Where should we run the ad?

After this discussion, the agency writes the creative brief, the document that serves as a roadmap for the project. It ensures that both client and agency are on the same page as to what this particular ad is meant to accomplish, who the target audience is, and other details about what is expected. Once the agency writes this creative brief, both the agency and the storeowner sign off on it, which indicates everyone is in agreement.

Most Profitable Retailers don't employ an ad agency for their stores, but you can still adapt some of an ad agency's best practices – such as making a creative brief – in order to make your marketing materials better targeted. Taking an hour or so to get everything down on paper can save hours of time down the road – not to mention wasted dollars – since you and your staff (and whatever outsiders may be involved) will have the project spelled out for them.

For the back-to-school shoe store ad, here are some questions the creative brief will answer: Are we targeting moms, or the students themselves? When will the ad run? When do schools in this area open? Are we offering a coupon? How big is the ad? What is our budget? Do we need to take photos? What is the publication's deadline for ads? Will it run once or more often? How will we know the ad is effective?

Looks like one simple ad isn't so simple after all. That's why Profitable Retailers answer all the questions up front, before anyone devotes any time to the project. It's easy – frighteningly so – to waste marketing dollars, and that's why a creative brief will get you off on the right foot and guide you throughout the process of creating a new marketing piece, whether it's an ad, a newsletter, or even new business cards.

There are plenty of templates for creative briefs online – some simple, and some much more complex. The following model provides a creative brief starting point. As you follow your creative brief, you can modify it according to what works best for you.

While writing their creative briefs, Profitable Retailers answer these questions:

- *Who is the target?*

- *What do they think of us?*

- *What do we want them to know?*

- *What data do we have to back up what we're saying?*

- *How will we know this program works?*

- *What's the best format?*

- *What's the budget?*

You may find that in writing the creative brief, what you want to do is bigger than your wallet allows. But it's good to get a sense of the task at hand and the scope of the project before you begin.

The Question: What do you want your marketing materials to accomplish? Or, put another way, when a potential customer reads your marketing message, what do you want that person to do?

Taking a Flier on Flyers

One of the oldest forms of advertising is a poster announcing a special event. You may be called on to create a poster (flyer) if your store is having a social gathering, special seminar, or other event that requires publicity. Whether creating an oversized poster or flyers printed on 8 1/2- by 11-inch paper, Profitable Retailers want to make the most out of the space available. Here are some tips to keep in mind when creating your next flyer:

Choose your biggest words carefully. Just like a billboard on a highway, your flyer has a split-second to attract a reader to stop and read more. Instead of putting your store's name as the biggest words on the page, think of which words will attract the most people. This might be *"Free Seminar"* or *"Meet Other Knitters"* or *"Free Fashion Show."* Whatever you end up using, the biggest words should be the most important point. Don't waste the big type on words that will not attract a prospect's attention.

Keep the typeface simple. It's tempting to use a fun typeface (font) for a flyer; however, keep in mind that your goal is to make this flyer as readable as possible. Some fonts are just too difficult to read. It's better to stick with a less interesting typeface that's clean and easy to read — even at a glance. Also, don't fall into the trap of using multiple typefaces on the same page. Your flyer won't look "fun" – it will be a jumbled mess. If you want to use variations in typeface, use boldface and italic of the same typeface for variety.

Go easy with the clip art. Just as you want typefaces to be clean and simple, you want your artwork to be simple, too. When you've located usable clip art (much is available free online), it's tempting to want to use it all – from the Pilgrim hat to the turkey and pumpkins right through to the scarecrow and shocks of wheat. It's true that a piece of artwork could add a nice touch to your flyer, but use it only if it adds something and not just to "decorate" the piece.

Who, what, where, when, why? Make sure the reader can find all the information that's necessary from this poster or flyer. Include the date(s), time(s), admission or ticket prices, and a summary of events ("Seminar starts at 3 p.m. with hot dogs and soda at 6 p.m."). If the event is free, don't assume people will know that; make sure that information is available. Also, offer a way to obtain more information such as a phone number or a website. You will likely just have one chance to get the person to commit so you want to answer all the questions at once.

Double- and triple-check. This may sound crazy, but always double- and triple-check the date. Businesses issue announcements or invitations all the time with the wrong dates. They'll announce that the event is "Tuesday, August 4" when August 4 is really a Wednesday that year. These errors are followed by a corrected announcement, which causes confusion and makes the business appear disorganized. It's such a simple item to get right, but it's human nature not to check it. Before you start printing any flyer, verify the day and date on an actual calendar. Then have someone check the date without you. This will take less than a minute and is worth every second.

Find a test subject. Profitable Retailers know it's always a good idea to test any piece of marketing material on someone unfamiliar with it. Take a moment to have a friend or someone from the business next door look at it. You'll be surprised by the misunderstandings or the amount of information you may have left out. What you think "everyone knows" might be something that you need to include on the flyer. Having someone review the flyer will just take a few minutes. That person might ask, "Are the hot dogs free?" Having your flyer checked can prevent misunderstandings.

Distribution, distribution, distribution... Once you've designed your flyer, be generous in its distribution. Hang them all over your store – even in the restroom. Use them as bag-stuffers or self-mailers. The point is to get as many people to see the flyer as possible. Think about other outlets for distribution such as churches or clubs in your area.

The Question: What can you do to make your flyers more effective?

Beep Beep! Time to
Tune Up the Website

You do have a website, don't you? In the mid-'90s, a store that had a website was considered a trendsetter since sites were still a novelty for many businesses. As Internet culture and commerce has evolved, you no longer have the luxury of not having a website. Customers assume all businesses have sites. It's that simple.

A website could be nothing more than your store's description, address, phone, fax, and email address along with directions to the store. A few photographs of your store in action round out the basics of a "starter" site. These days, when customers want to know more about a business, they are not going to look at the Yellow Pages – these customers will check you out online, and that happens twenty-fours hours a day, seven days a week.

Profitable Retailers don't neglect their websites, even during a store's busy period. You may not have time for a complete overhaul, but you can do a few things to make sure that your site is "visitor ready." Here are some suggestions:

Add some headlines and subheads. Most people skim a

web page looking for something that interests them or for the particular information they're seeking. Copy that doesn't look that long when it's printed on a page or on your computer screen could be much too long for a web page. See if you have any large blocks of copy that should be broken up by subheads. (A subhead is a headline within the body of a story.) There may be places where you can add attention to your words by adding a subhead.

Toot your own horn. Think about what's unique about your store. What do you do better than anyone else? Whatever that is – whether it's your merchandise selection, your new rental equipment, your special gift-wrap, or your expertise – make sure that positive aspect of your business is prominently displayed.

Have a good supply of content. Don't fall into the trap of believing that you don't have enough material for a website. Quotes from happy customers are terrific to post on your site. You may be surprised at how flattered a customer would be if asked for a testimonial. While you're at it, post their photo, too. Testimonials carry tremendous credibility. Your customers may describe an aspect of your store, a good experience, or just their overall opinion of your operation.

Update, update, update. Take a quick look to make sure all staff members mentioned are still your employees. Make sure all dates are current. It's common on retail sites to see "End of Summer Sale" in November or "Valentine's Day Specials" in April. Out-of-date information frustrates your site's visitors and makes the rest of the information on your site appear questionable.

Double-check the inner workings of your site. Programming glitches can make navigation between the pages of your site impossible at times. Make sure you can click on and go to all sections of your site. If you have external links, make sure they still work.

Mention your store's special benefits. Are there any benefits that you may take for granted that should be on your site? Maybe you have a bilingual staff member, for example. It's easy to forget that some of the things that are everyday business for you are plusses for your customers. This is not time to be modest about you or your staff.

The Internet is the 21ˢᵗ century phonebook. More and more, people use the Internet as a phonebook. Make sure that your street address, telephone number, and email address are on the opening page of your site. A customer at work who needs to call you might find it easier to quickly check your site for your phone number than to look you up in the phone book.

The Question: When was the last time you reviewed your website?

Making News Without Being in the Police Blotter

If you've ever wondered how to get an article about your store in the local media or featured on your local radio and television stations, it's easier than you think.

Profitable Retailers know that the best way to get stories about their stores published in magazines and newspapers is by having bona fide news the editor thinks will be of interest to a publication's readers (or to radio or television stations' listeners and viewers). Issuing news releases with real news on a consistent and timely basis develops a reputation for you and your store as a good news source.

Another way to increase your store's coverage is to anticipate what an editor will need during the year. How do you do that? Part of it's common sense. Think about the kind of stories your local newspaper covers throughout the year.

For example: Most newspapers have a feature article in late November or early December about unique holiday gifts. The writer of this yearly article will always be on the lookout for additional interesting gifts to include. By providing the newspaper with information about your store's holiday offerings, you will be supplying useful information while at the same time increasing the odds that your store will be mentioned.

What else? Some newspapers may highlight a particular business each week in Sunday's business section. Or a newspaper may run regular profiles of senior citizens doing interesting things – and you can supply the newspaper with information about one of your older staff members who began working with you after retiring from a different career. Look at the magazines and newspapers you would like your store to appear in, and see if you can find ways to match what's happening at your store with the needs of a particular publication.

When sending your news to a publication, don't assume that the publication will know why you're sending it. In the example of senior citizens profiles, include a note that says something to the effect of, "We thought Tom Smith would make an interesting person to feature in your 'Spotlight on Seniors' section."

Better yet, call the editor or writer who is responsible for the section and discuss your staff person's accomplishments. No doubt, the writer will ask you to send some information. Once you get that go ahead from the writer, you must act on it. Make sure the information gets to the writer within a few days – no longer than that. Nothing will help build a good relationship with an editor better than keeping your word about sending what you've promised on a timely basis.

Another way to increase your chances of getting publications to cover your business is by looking at the editorial calendars of the publications. Simply stated, an editorial calendar is a plan an editor makes for the year of the main articles or topics to be covered during the year. You can get an editorial calendar by requesting it by letter or telephone.

Once you have the calendar, study the publication's plans and see if anything happening at your store fits. In the case of a regional business magazine, you may receive the editorial calendar and see that, in the June issue, the magazine is planning a feature on women-owned businesses. If you're a woman-owned store, pick up the phone or write a letter and introduce yourself.

Whatever opportunities you see to get editorial coverage for your store, keep one crucial concept in mind: editors work on deadlines far in advance of when the publication comes out. The Sunday sections of a newspaper may be planned weeks in advance. A monthly magazine works three to four months ahead of the publication date, which means if you're aiming to be in the June issue of a magazine, you need to get your news in during March. For holiday coverage, start thinking about ideas after Labor Day. If you get in the habit of anticipating what an editor needs, you'll be able to get increased coverage for your store.

So, once you're ready to go, how do you craft a news release? Here's how to do it in five easy steps:

Step #1: Provide a reliable contact. At the top of your news release, include the name, telephone number, and email address of someone that an editor or producer can call to follow up or ask questions. This should be a person who is knowledgeable about the contents of the release, readily available should the media call, and comfortable discussing the issue with the media. The best person to list as a contact might be the person who wrote the news release or the person who is most familiar with the issue being discussed.

Step #2: Include the date of the news. Always put a date at the top of your news release. Reporters are often frustrated when a release simply states "for immediate release," which gives no indication of just how old the news contained in the release may be.

Few, if any, reasons exist for a store to ask for an "embargo" (asking the media to hold back on using your news release until a particular date and time that you specify). Embargoing a release may make your store look foolish to the editors and reporters who read it. You're not the White House with pressing news that must be held back for legal, security, or ethical reasons. Just put the current date at the top of the release so reporters will know how timely the issue may be when they get around to receiving and reading it a day or two later.

Step #3: Write a headline. Your headline should be centered on the page and communicate the essence of your entire news release. Write it in bold type, preferably in a size that's one or two points larger than your body copy. The reporter or editor receiving your news release may read nothing else, which is why it's crucial for your headline to convey your main message in an instant. It should be short and use action words that grab attention and make your release stand out from the hundreds of releases that are received daily.

Step #4: Write a lead paragraph. The next important element is your first, or lead, paragraph. Again, this should communicate the essence of the story, touching upon all the main points you wish to address. You can go into detail in the following paragraphs. If your headline is eye catching and grabs the attention of the editor or reporter, then your lead paragraph has to close the sale by conveying all the pertinent information that reporter will need to make a story decision. The remainder of your news release can provide the details of your story, but your first paragraph should touch on all the major facets, much as an executive summary does in a business report.

Step #5: Identify the news. Make sure your news release actually contains news. Today, when reporters and editors are barraged with literally hundreds of news releases daily, many releases find their way to the recycling bin before they are even opened. It's unrealistic to think that simply being open for business is news. Discounts for your customers may be good news for your customers, but it's not news for your local newspaper. Under most circumstances, redecorating or unveiling a new sign is not news. Be careful that you don't get a reputation for crying wolf with non-news among your local reporters.

Don't wait until you have the perfect list of all media to receive your release. Start sending your releases even if you have just a few contacts. Many publications include the email addresses of their writers and reporters so you can send an email news release directly to them. Don't abuse that privilege. Your job is to build a rapport with editors, not turn them off with useless email.

Profitable Retailers know that editors want real news. That's first and foremost. News releases that are actually promotional pieces or advertising copy for your store will not be used. New jobs, new buildings, special events, community participation, charitable acts, business growth, a visiting dignitary – these topics all have news potential. Being in business is not enough to warrant news coverage. Develop a consciousness about the newsworthy happenings at your store so that you can react with a news release. If you're not sure, study the newspapers or magazines where you'd like to be covered and become familiar with the articles and news that they use.

The Question: What is newsworthy at your store?

Low-tech Solutions in a High-tech World

Not all marketing has to be innovative or state-of-the-art. There are ways to attract customers to your store that have worked for decades. A surefire marketing strategy is helium-filled balloons with your store logo on them. Believe it or not, it's one of the best dollar-for-dollar marketing strategies you can invest in. Balloons expose your store to hundreds of people, they stay in the customers' homes for days, they bring smiles to faces, they make you feel good, and – most important – balloons require a minimal investment of time and money.

Think about it. Every weekend – or day of the week, for that matter – you decorate the front of your store with balloons. First of all, customers think you must be having a special event or sale, so they come in. Every child is attracted to balloons like nails to a magnet. The child pulls the parent toward the store to see the balloons. The first thing you or your staff does (because, of course, someone is near the door to welcome everyone who comes in) is give a balloon to the child, who then responds with a big smile. The parent will immediately think more favorably of you and your store. As the child plays with the balloon, the parent might even choose to spend more time shopping in the store on that visit. But wait – the payoff is just beginning.

The family leaves and continues to walk around the shopping area, exposing your store's name to more potential customers. The impact is even greater when people see multiple families walking around with balloons. When they walk by your store, they associate the balloons they've seen other people carrying around with the balloons you have in front of your store and – presto! – in they come. And it doesn't end there. As a parent, I've found out the hard way that getting children to throw out a balloon before it's down to the size of a golf ball can be difficult. So your balloon ends up in someone's home for at least a couple of days, exposing the parent, child, and any guests they might have to your logo.

Profitable Retailers know that while all the exposure is great, ultimately the best reason to execute a balloon strategy is the joy it brings to the child. And one thing I've learned in my life, the more I try to improve the lives of others, the more my life improves.

You can rent large helium tanks from gas suppliers or welding supply companies. Secure the tank against a wall in the back room; two eye hooks with a chain going across will ensure it doesn't fall and hurt anyone. Invest in logo balloons. While giving out generic balloons is a nice thing to do, it doesn't give you the quality exposure you're also seeking. And do it religiously. If you decide to hand out balloons every Saturday and Sunday, then do it every Saturday and Sunday.

The Question: How would being known as "the nice place that gives out balloons" help your sales?

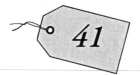

Emailing for Fun and Profits

Unsolicited email is becoming increasingly annoying to everyone – including your customers. It's estimated that nearly one out of every three emails received is unsolicited by the recipient – the email known as spam. Millions of these messages are sent every day. For a small business, such as a retail store wishing to communicate via email, the proliferation of spam can make getting your message read more challenging as customers aggressively filter out spam or click the delete button.

Here are some ways that Profitable Retailers make sure their bona fide marketing messages are read by their customers and not deleted along with messages for "Male Enhancement" and "Miracle Weight Loss":

Get your customers' permission. Your customers want to stay informed as to sales and special events at your store, so the majority of them will willingly give you their email addresses. By getting permission to send them email, you will not only show you respect their privacy, but they will also be aware that you may be sending them important information.

Permission can come from a website sign up, a current email communication, in-person during a phone conversation, or an in-store sign-up sheet or meeting. Some companies then send a "double opt-in" email, which confirms the permission received by your store to send email to that address. Make sure that the sign-up mechanism for your newsletter or mailing list is prominently displayed on your homepage. Don't miss the opportunity to capture a visitor's email address by hiding it somewhere on your site.

Stick to business. Everyone receives patriotic, inspirational, or amusing emails that circulate around the Internet. Your best bet is to resist the temptation to pass these along to your customers. The more popular of these have probably already been sent to your customers numerous times. Show that you respect their email privacy by keeping your communications to business and store topics.

Choose your subject line carefully. Don't compose your subject line in a last-second rush – or worse – leave it completely blank. The subject line is what will entice the recipient to open your email or to delete it without reading. It's a good idea to keep some consistency in your subject lines, thereby training your customers to recognize your correspondences. For example, you might put as a subject line: "ABC Store: Special January Clearance," followed by "ABC Store: Last-Minute Bargains," followed by "ABC Store: Meet the Author Night." Identify your store and give the recipient a good reason to open the email.

Avoid being filtered out. Many customers use spam filters that separate what the software perceives as spam from other email. One way the filters work is by identifying common words used in spam. You might think that "ABC Store: Save $$$ Now" is a good subject line, but the "Save $$$" part could get your email filtered out as spam. Some other filtered words and phrases are "money-back guarantee," "advertisement," "order now," and "adults only." A complete list of filtered words is available at

Microsoft's website. It's worth checking out so that you avoid using these combinations of words.

Don't send attachments. Well-placed concern about receiving a virus makes many people wary about opening any attachment. If you want to show a spectacular photo of a new product or a schedule of classes, post it on your website and provide a hot link (a URL recipients can click on) that will take them to the site.

Have a privacy policy. Profitable Retailers have a strict privacy policy, which means never selling or sharing their customer email list with anyone. This policy is essential to retain the trust of your customers. Email communication builds trust and cultivates business. With dozens of spam emails arriving in their inboxes, your customers will appreciate your personalized messages and their attention to detail.

Devise an official system. Have a system in place whereby you designate who can email your customers in bulk. A sales associate might email an individual customer to tell her that a special order has arrived, for example, but you should formalize who on your staff is allowed to email customers. This sounds basic, but just as you wouldn't permit just anyone to send out a news release with your store's name on it, you need to identify who has the authority to email the bulk customer list. By limiting the access to your customers' email addresses, you may also avoid the mistake of accidentally emailing your customers inappropriate messages intended for internal use only.

Go easy with the number of messages. If you don't have a defined schedule for sending out email communication to your customers such as a "Friday Newsletter," decide in advance how often you think is appropriate for sending these emails. Two or three times a month is a reasonable schedule for sending messages. You don't want your emails to become so frequent that they become irritating to the very people you're trying to woo.

The Question: Are you taking advantage of email to market to your customers?

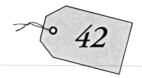

The Star of Your Advertising Campaign: You!

You're the best advertisement your store can have. You're in the community, attending functions, talking to people, and generally being visible to potential customers. Some people are turned off by the topic of "networking"; the word makes them envision some fast-talking salesman shoving business cards in their hand as they try to navigate the buffet table. Profitable Retailers can network less aggressively, but just as effectively by being a walking billboard for their store. Here are some ways to do that:

Wear clothing with your store logo on it. Don't think you have to be a huge store in order to have shirts with the store's name on them. Even if your shop consists of you and one other person, you can buy a limited quantity of shirts with your store's name or logo embroidered on it. In addition to having your name out in the community every day, the store shirt will provide a consistent and neat appearance for you and your staff.

Create an attractive nametag. You attend events all year long where you're presented with the sticker nametag on which you're supposed to write your name with a magic marker. Do something different. You can have an attractive, high-quality, permanent nametag made to wear at community events and meetings outside your store. These nametags can be ordered through any advertising specialty company. You'll forget you're wearing it after a while, and your visibility in the community will soar.

Have some good photos of yourself taken. Most folks don't enjoy having their photograph taken, which means there are no good photos on hand. Presenting yourself as the personification of your store demonstrates to customers that you "walk the walk." If you own a garden store, have some photos taken in your own garden. If you own a bookstore, have a photo taken of you reading. Profitable Retailers will use these photos for brochures, media requests, or their store's newsletter. If you do this often, you will become accustomed to having your photo taken and will have a selection of photos on hand so you're not using the same photo over and over. Although you probably require a corporate "headshot" taken by a professional photographer, action shots (even if the "action" is gardening or reading) are more interesting.

Carry business cards. Five hundred business cards gathering dust in their original box in the bottom drawer of your desk are worthless. No cheaper promotion piece exists than a business card, so hand them out liberally. Don't just use them in formal business situations. If your business card is dull and lifeless, design a new one that will work for you. Profitable Retailers make business cards more than a piece of cardstock with their name and phone number on it. You could include something like, "Call about our monthly trips to [destination]!" or "Learn to cook in five weeks!" Make having a supply of interesting business cards a priority, and you just may drum up some new business.

Hand out coupons or discount certificates. In addition to a business card, you might also consider handing out a discount certificate for new visitors to your store or a coupon for a free item. The "free item" doesn't have to be merchandise – it could be nothing more than a fact sheet that customers may find useful. If you own a toy store, your fact sheet could be a list of toys appropriate for different age groups. If you own a camera store, your fact sheet could provide ten tips for purchasing a digital camera, or a glossary of photographic terms. If you own a beauty supply store, you could provide a fact sheet of color trends for the year or cosmetic tips for women of different age groups. Use your expertise to woo customers to your store.

Be prepared to talk about your store. When you're standing in line at McDonald's wearing your store shirt and a fellow diner asks you about your store, be prepared with an answer that's more than "We're down the street," or "It's just a store." Profitable Retailers pull out a business card and give a ten-second sales pitch about the joys of their stores. The more often you do it, the more comfortable you'll become.

The Question: Are you a good advertisement for your own store?

And You Can Quote Me on That

You read quotes from experts in newspapers and magazines every day. A school psychologist may comment on some aspect of children's behavior, a lawyer may briefly explain a new law, or a wine shop owner may offer advice on the perfect wines to serve with various food selections. Journalists rely on expert testimony to add real-world credibility to articles as well as a touch of human interest. Because experts add so much to articles, journalists are always on the lookout for new ones to interview and quote. Profitable Retailers make terrific experts!

You don't have to have a Masters or a PhD – in fact, you don't have to have any special education to be considered an expert. A 13-year-old girl is an expert on what 13-year-old girls consider cool. Someone could be an expert on beer, local history, gardening, model trains, liver diseases – virtually any topic you can think of.

As a Profitable Retailer, you're an expert, too. You're an expert on retail operations, sales, and customer service. But it goes beyond that. You may also be an expert on employing college students, local beaches, airline travel, holiday decorations, gift wrapping, sunglasses, minimum wage laws... The list goes on and on. Take some time to think about what you're an expert on. Don't be modest; you probably know more than you think.

To position yourself as an expert, you need to get your timing down. Calling a local reporter to announce that you're a retail sales expert might garner a ho-hum response. But announcing yourself as knowledgeable about the impact of new parking in the downtown area while your town is deciding whether to build a parking garage makes sense. You're definitely an expert when a writer is creating a story about holiday sales.

Generating positive publicity for your store by acknowledging your own expertise is easier than you think. You don't even have to leave your store. One good technique is to respond to an article you've read. Most publications publish writers' email addresses either in the masthead (near the front of the publication) or at the end of the story.

You may say nothing more than, "I enjoyed reading your story about hiring seasonal help. My own experience has been..." or "Your review of adult education classes was nearly complete. However, you left out one of the most popular classes in town..." Keep your comments brief and informal. In your response, include a description of who you are, what background makes you an expert ("I've taught more than a hundred classes on scrap-booking..." or "I've hired college students to work summers for a dozen years..."), and your opinions or comments.

Don't forget to include your signature line in the email. A signature line contains standard contact information: your name, phone, fax, email, store name, address, website URL, etc. If you don't hear anything back right away, don't become discouraged. Keep at it, though, and you'll be contacted by a writer who thinks your expertise will help an article he or she is writing.

Whether you're contacted after an outgoing email or whether a reporter or writer contacts you on their own, make certain you reply in a timely manner. Reporters are always on deadline, so make getting in touch with them a priority. The overwhelming majority of media calls to you will result in positive publicity for your store. By planting seeds in the media, you can make the process happen that much faster.

The Question: In what areas are you an expert? How can you use this knowledge to market your store?

Is it Done Yet? Ending the Never-ending Project.

One of the major enemies of finishing a promotional project is the inability to let go of it. Companies sometimes take a year (or more!) to complete a brochure and get it to the printer. Sounds ridiculous, right? But it happens; here's how:

For your new brochure, you decide you need some photos taken at your last customer appreciation party. By next week the store will be decorated for Halloween and you also want photos of that. You want to include information about your partnership with a local health club, but the deal hasn't been signed yet. A key employee is leaving, and you don't want to picture the replacement until you see if she works out. On top of all of this, there are rumors that your area code is going to change (*again*), and you don't want to publish the wrong phone number. That's how a brochure can take a year or more to go to print.

Here's a good concept to keep in mind: the perfect newsletter, brochure, handout, or flyer doesn't exist. No matter how much hard work you put into a project, you will always find a way to do it differently. Sometimes the changes you want will make the project better; sometimes the changes are nothing more than changes.

Have you ever caught yourself using any of these excuses?

"I want it to be perfect." Everyone wants a brochure or newsletter to be the best it can possibly be. The problem with striving for perfection is that it's an impossible goal. Every project entails a little compromise. Don't get so hung up on trying to produce the perfect publication that you waste time that could be spent having a very good end product.

"Let's look at it one more time." The desire to look at a piece one more time can be minimized if you have a system in place for proofreading and approving. In a system where individuals are held accountable (because their participation is evident or they've signed off on the piece), you can get the product to the printer, knowing that six sets of eyes and six brains have been involved in the final approval process.

Sure, sometimes looking at your publication one more time may improve it if you catch an error, but it's more likely that the desire to look at something again is just a stalling technique. Make sure that management, selected sales staff, and maybe your bookkeeper are included in the process. When people with different interests look at a piece, they will look at different aspects of it.

"Does this sound better?" Who knows? You can waste days trying to figure out if one word sounds better than another. "Quilting is really fun." "Quilting is a lot of fun." Does it really make a difference? Probably not. And even if there's a difference, that difference is probably not worth making the piece two weeks late in order to make the change. Here's a rule that will save you countless headaches: any change has to improve the piece, not just provide an alternate way of writing something.

There's a Japanese proverb applicable to this situation: *The perfect is the enemy of the good.* Be happy with a "good" product that's actually finished rather than to try in vain for a "perfect" product.

"Should the lawyer look it over?" Your lawyer probably doesn't have to read your "Valentine's Day Merchandise Has Arrived" bag-stuffer before it's printed. However, you will want your lawyer to read the employee handbook before it goes to print. Profitable Retailers decide ahead of time which individuals will be involved in the creation of a piece and decide when in the process their input or approval should come.

"Should we add something about our Frequent Buyer program?" What starts out as a postcard can end up as an eight-page brochure if you're not careful. Add something about an open house. List the staff. Provide a map to the store. Add your email address. There might be a sentence about being kid-friendly. But always keep yourself focused on the goal of the piece.

"We just want to sit with it for a while." This is a vague reason for some underlying problem with the piece. After all, a brochure or newsletter is not cheese or wine; neither are going to get better with age. When you're tempted to say, "Let's just sit with it for a while," ask yourself what the real problem is with the piece. It's better to identify a potential problem and get it out in the open than to have your piece die of old age day-by-day, while sapping little bits of energy out of you daily as you think about it.

Even after you get your piece to the printer, you're still not finished. Profitable Retailers still have to answer that tough question: "How many should we print?" It's so tempting to go with the larger amount when the incremental costs between printing 300 and 500 are so small. It's scary to think about running out of brochures or holiday handouts. If you're like most businesses though, you've probably thrown out more printed pieces that are out of date than you like to think about. The more time sensitive a piece is, the fewer you'll need. For example, if you're inviting 200 customers to a party, you don't need 500 invitations. However, if a piece is evergreen – such as a brochure about your store's offerings – think of it as having a useful shelf life of about two years. Then figure out how many you'll use in that time frame.

The Question: Do you have a system in place for timely production of promotional items?

Operations

The day-to-day procedures you set up in your store will have a major impact on your bottom line. Profitable Retailers know that each day presents new challenges and opportunities to improve the systems at work in their stores.

Checking Your Checklist

One way an airplane pilot maintains a smooth operation is to employ checklists, which are carried for different parts of the flight. A pilot uses a checklist to inspect the airplane prior to take off. Referring to this printed checklist means that it is less likely that an item will be overlooked. There's safety in it, too – pilots don't have to depend on memory; they just take out their checklist and go through each item.

Profitable Retailers, like proficient pilots, know checklists are great tools. Providing a checklist for your sales associates to use prior to the store opening is an easy way to make sure that all tasks are done each day. Even if one sales associate doesn't complete all the tasks required for opening the store, each task can be individually assigned. Having a checklist also makes these tasks rote; no judgment is required and each item can be ticked off the list once completed.

Of course, the tasks to be completed prior to opening or closing are going to vary from store to store. The following are tasks that are appropriate for most stores. The timely completion of these tasks each day might take no more than fifteen minutes, but their completion will lay the groundwork for a more efficient and less stressful day on the sales floor.

Vacuum every day. Even if you don't vacuum the entire store, run the vacuum around the front door (hear all those little bits being sucked up?), in front of the cash register, the dressing rooms, and other major traffic areas. A thorough vacuuming can be done weekly.

Check cash register supplies. Make sure that bags, tissue paper, register tape, credit card slips, staples, etc., are at the ready. This is also a good way to make sure you never run out of a particular component while ringing up a sale. You will never be caught in the middle of a busy sales period and realize there's no register tape in the store.

Check for sufficient stock on display. This doesn't call for a mini-inventory every day. It means checking for "holes" or gaps that catch your eye on the floor. This is another good way to determine when restocking is necessary.

Do a quick scan for damaged or soiled merchandise. Walking through the store will show whether anything sticks out that has makeup stains, rips, tears, loose buttons, missing price tags, etc. Anything not deemed appropriate for the sales floor can be removed, repaired, and, if possible, returned for sale.

Refold. This is the bane of many salespeople. If you stock folded shirts, a customer may have grabbed one and just put it back on the pile. See if anything needs to be refolded or neatened to give your store a polished look.

Check the dressing rooms. Merchandise may have been inadvertently left in the dressing room. Not only is this unsightly, it's a security risk that makes shoplifting easier. If you don't know what is in that room, you won't miss it until it's too late. Make sure you start the day with spotless dressing rooms.

Do a quick size sort. This does not mean a total rearranging of items on hangers. Customers move things during the sales day, so take a minute or two to put the sizes (or colors or styles) back together where they belong. Make sure all hangers are placed the same way on a rack.

Dress your mannequins. If you use mannequins in your displays, make sure they are still fully dressed with whatever gear they are supposed to be sporting and that all tags are out of sight.

Do a quick Windexing. Give a quick swipe to the front door and the glass cabinet tops and fronts. It's a good rule to not use cleaners when customers are present. The beauty of doing it daily is that the surfaces can never get too dirty. If a finger mark or blotch is missed on Monday, you'll get it on Tuesday.

With a checklist, everything will get done each day. Sales associates can divide the tasks among themselves to "fly" through the checklist and get ready to open the front door.

The Question: Are you using checklists for smooth operations?

Chart Your Course on Monday

"Monday, Monday" by The Mamas & the Papas, begins with, "Monday, Monday, so good to me, / Monday, Monday, it was all I hoped it would be…"

I couldn't agree more. Years ago I developed the habit of spending the first part of Monday morning reviewing the results of the past week and then preparing for the upcoming week. To be a Profitable Retailer, you must spend time thinking and planning your business and not just running it.

Another way of looking at this is that you want to spend time working *on* your business instead of simply working *in* your business. It's way too easy to be swallowed up by the day's events when you become no more than your own employee. In other words, the captain of the ship doesn't swab the decks; he instructs others to do it while he charts the course.

I have found the best way to work *on* your business is to spend Monday morning answering a series of questions. If you're an owner/operator, I recommend that you write out the answers in a notebook or on a document on your computer. Don't get caught up in creating the perfect journal or spreadsheet, though. That's just another way to procrastinate. If you work more efficiently in a spiral notebook, use that. Any notebook will do. If you're comfortable with a keyboard and a computer screen, create a document for yourself. But stick to the situation at hand rather than getting caught up in color coding columns or finding the perfect typeface.

Keeping a history of your answers is a valuable tool that you may use from time to time. If you have store managers who work for you, I recommend they send you answers to these questions sometime on Monday. Of course, the managers may balk, but it's up to you to set the tone for how crucial an understanding of the numbers is for your operation. It won't take long – a few weeks, in fact – to develop a history that even recalcitrant managers may find interesting. And it wouldn't hurt to add a small dose of competition to the mix.

Whether it's just you answering these questions or you're relying on others to supply data, bear in mind that perfect spelling and grammar, fancy language, and perfectly formatted documents are not required. You want to write in your own words and provide accurate data. Resist, too, the temptation to gild the lily – that is, if things are bad, say so. This is not time to look on the bright side. Like Sergeant Friday on *Dragnet*, you just want "the facts, ma'am."

Here are some questions to get you started:

Where are you in relation to your sales goal for the week, the month, and the year? It's important to always know how you're doing against your goal. I know this sounds incredibly simple, but you would be amazed how many people actually don't know this when you ask them. In fact, you would be surprised at how many people don't even have goals! Reviewing this every Monday will ensure that you and your store managers know your performance to date. All other decisions stem from these results.

What three things are working? It's important to look at your strengths each week. These are the areas of your business that drive positive results in your business. Don't limit yourself when answering this question. They could be certain products, merchandising methods, advertisements, promotions, employee contests, certain employees, and just about anything else in your business.

Remember, you're writing for posterity, and your memory might not hold out. Be specific with your answers. Instead of writing, "Our direct mail program started netting some sales," write, "We had fifty-six customers redeem coupons this week from the Mother's Day ad."

What three things are not working? This area is especially important if you're falling short of your sales goals. Look for areas that are either truly impacting your results or at least have the potential to make a negative impact. Try to avoid listing answers that are really only minor nuisances – unless they are impacting staff morale. Forcing yourself to uncover three each week helps you discover small problem areas before they become big.

An example of what may not be working is, "Main access to the parking lot has been blocked by road construction for two days," or "No customer has mentioned ad in Sunday paper – and we were asking!"

Looking forward to the coming week, here are three questions to ask:

What two or three actions can you take this week to build upon what's working? It's one thing to identify what's working, but success and profits come from improving on that knowledge. If a certain marketing campaign is working, you may explore its expansion. It's important to write down *action items* that can be worked on during the week. Not what you would like to do, not what you're thinking about doing, but what you *will* do. Examples of action items might be: "Contact newspaper sales rep to check price for larger ad," or "Continue to offer free gift wrapping." Your first steps might be to contact someone to determine what it would cost to expand upon something you're already doing. The key to profits and success is action!

What two or three actions can you take today to improve areas from the "things not working" list? One of the advantages of preparing this report weekly is the fact that if you don't take action on your problems, they will continue to appear on the list. There's nothing worse than writing down or reading about the same problem week after week. You'll find great joy in the ability to take action and move an item from the not working to what's working section! German writer and philosopher Johann von Goethe once said, "Knowing is not enough; we must apply. Willing is not enough; we must do." I think Johann might have also made a pretty good Profitable Retailer!

What will you, as the leader of your team or organization, do this week to improve the lives of your staff? Ultimately, your success hinges on the interaction between two human beings on the retail floor. Those two people are your customer and your employee. It's critical to your success that your employees be happy, passionate, and focused on the customer. That can only happen if they feel that you feel the same way about them. Once again, it's action that drives results.

Good planning is necessary to capitalize on your opportunities, overcome your challenges, and maximize your profits. Maybe The Mamas & the Papas were talking about profits when they sang, "Oh Monday morning, Monday morning couldn't guarantee, / That Monday evening you would still be here with me…" There are no guarantees that you'll be profitable, but spending Monday mornings focused on analyzing your current situation puts you that much closer to being a really Profitable Retailer.

The Question: Will you spend next Monday working on your business?

Back to the Basics

Wouldn't it be great if we could wave a magic wand, sprinkle fairy dust, or twitch our nose like Samantha on *Bewitched* to create the perfect retail environment? So far, those techniques only work in books and on television, not real life. No magic is going to transform us into Profitable Retailers.

What will work, though, is far less glamorous. What works is knowing and applying retail basics to your particular store. It's neither exciting nor sexy, but the basics work. When a sports team is stuck in a losing streak, what does the coach say? He usually claims that the team is going to "get back to the basics" with practice drills to reverse the trend. When your child's teacher is concerned about your son or daughter's progress, one of the remedies typically involves "getting back to the basics."

So how are your retail basics? Are you and your employees executing the basics? While the basics aren't as sexy as a big initiative, they do determine *your* wins and losses, sales, profits, and customer satisfaction. Here are a few basics that Profitable Retailers have made standard operating procedure:

Clean storefronts. The storefront is the entry point of your customer's experience. It's important to keep doors and windows free of fingerprints *throughout* the day, not just before the store opens. Are the doors and windows free of old tape? If you use an "Open" sign, is the right side turned out at opening time? Are the ledges wiped down, both inside and outside the store? Most people miss that outside ledge thinking it's the landlord's responsibility to clean it. Whether it is or it isn't, it's part of your customer's experience.

Straight signs. I would guess that over fifty percent of the stores, both chain and independent, I visit have crooked signs. Are signs easy to hang? No. Do crooked signs really look that bad? Well, it's not as bad as dirty floors and empty boxes around the store, but it's a basic that can and should be executed well. (You do want to beat your version of the Yankees, don't you?)

Staff appearance. Set the bar high and keep it there. This is one of those basics that stores can slowly drift away from. I'm pretty sure that when the customer sees an unshaven male employee they don't wonder if he's unshaven because he has "sensitive skin." Frankly, they probably don't think about it much at all. But each element adds to the overall store impression and the appearance of your employees is an element of that. Keep your bar high. Be willing to send staff home if they don't meet your standards. This is one of the basics, where once you've set your standard, you don't have to work to keep it up, you just have to maintain your expectations.

Greeting the customer. This is not an option if you plan to be a successful business. Winning teams have a strategy for ensuring that every customer is greeted and is delivered the best possible experience. The busier the store, the more important it is to execute this well.

Leading on the floor. How can you or your managers coach the staff if time isn't spent on the floor? Working on the floor allows an owner or manager to watch the staff execute the basics. They are then in a position to praise strong performance and develop areas that need improvement.

Try to remember the last time a member of your store's management said to an employee, "You did a great job with the customer. I really liked when you [insert store-specific behavior], and I think you can [insert store-specific behavior] even better." What follows should be a basic you don't hear or see enough. "Now watch me [insert store-specific behavior] with this customer walking in."

To be a strong floor leader, you need at least three sets of eyes. You need to watch your different staff members working with customers, the activity at the sales counter, and for customers walking in. Always review what's working and what's not in the store, looking for small details that can be improved, and of course, giving the customer your undivided attention. Those of you who do it well know exactly what I'm saying.

Each one of these basics by themselves won't impact whether you win or lose the game, but added together, these and your other basics determine whether you're stuck in the cellar, the wildcard team, or the division clincher.

The Question: How are your basics? Are you doing what it takes to win every day?

A Clean Store is a Happy Store – and a Profitable One

One of the easiest facelifts you can give your store costs little or no money... Clean it! Being told to keep your store clean is a lot like your dentist telling you to floss. We all know we should do it. We all know it's good for us, but when the time crunch is on, the only way it's going to get done is to make it a priority.

What is clean anyway? Clean is more than an absence of dirt and dust, although that's a good place to start. Clean means your store looks good, feels good, and smells good. Clean sparkles. Clean shines. Clean makes your customers want to stay longer, to touch, to linger. Clean makes you smile. Clean makes your store a better place to work.

"Wait a minute," you say, "my store is supposed to smell good, too?" Yes, and if you sell perfumes, scented candles, and potpourri, it's easy to have a sweet-smelling store. Same thing if your store is a bakery. But what if you own a bike store? Or a bridal shop? How do you make sure your store smells good?

Just in case there's someone reading this book who still smokes, don't do it in your store. Never. Ever. Another way is by not eating in a store. Food smells can linger long after the food is gone. No one wants to smell your tuna salad or your French fries. The air in a store can become stale. If you have access to the outdoors, open a window or keep the front door open every so often to let some fresh air in. Ask others how your store smells. They may look at you funny, but you may be so used to your store that you can't smell it anymore. Regular carpet cleanings can help the air quality in a store, too.

Did you ever think that a messy store could lose you business? Consider how you miss a sale because your backroom is so disorganized that you can't find the size or color of a certain product a customer needs. Think of the money sitting in inventory because you inadvertently order product you already have. Think of the lost business when your salesperson spends ten minutes looking for the bright yellow item while the customer cools his heels (as well as his interest) and makes a bigger mess rummaging through boxes for the certain item that he knows is back there somewhere.

If you discourage customers from using your restroom because you're using it as an adjunct storeroom or maybe because it's just plain gross, the customer has no choice but to stop shopping and head home. Maybe never to return. You never know. This money you're losing is coming straight off your bottom line.

Just like with any aspect of store management, Profitable Retailers know that developing good routines is crucial. You need a plan. In fact, when it comes to housekeeping, stores often require more detailed planning than a typical office. That's because traffic flow in a store can vary greatly from day-to-day depending on sales, on-site events, holidays, and weather. Store hours may vary from day-to-day. When keeping the store clean is "everyone's job," it becomes the job of no one in particular. So get yourself a system for routinely cleaning your store – the big jobs and the small ones – and then stick with it.

By the way, don't just clean – declutter! No matter how clean your store is, it won't look its best until you get rid of that clutter. How many of the following clutterbugs are hanging out in your store waiting to get tossed?

- Outdated product catalogs

- Spare key to no one knows what

- Single boot whose mate has been missing for two years

- Register tape from your former cash register

- Unclaimed sweater

- Old Chamber of Commerce membership plaque

- Broken stapler

- Business cards with your old area code

- Post-it notes stuck to the cash register

- Pens that don't write

- Little packages of fast food ketchup and soy sauce

Cleaning your store regularly will go a long way to create a more pleasing sales environment. Once you're cleaning, you may see places where cleaning isn't enough. Part of what it takes to operate a well-run store is knowing when it's time to replace the carpet, buy new fixtures, and make other "infrastructure" updates. Did you know that vacuuming your carpeting regularly will extend its life? All those little bits of pebble and dirt wear the carpet down if they stay inside.

Having a clean store will do so much for you. A spanking clean store brightens your and your staff's outlook. Your customers will notice, too – they may not know why they're happier, but they'll sense the difference. When you make having a clean store a priority, you align that effort with your main priorities: customer service and sales. Once you have your systems in place, you and your staff will have forward motion that will create a momentum to keep the effort going. Plus, a clean, beautiful store is more fun to work in.

The Question: What's your system for making sure your store sparkles?

Don't Delay – Put It Away!

If you walk into any retail store, chances are good you'll see (or maybe even trip over) boxes of recently delivered merchandise. In the course of the day, you may get any number of deliveries – from the daily mail to boxes of new merchandise. When UPS arrives while you're with a customer, it's easy to just ask to have the packages left by the counter.

If you're busy, these recent deliveries get put over to the side until you can attend to them. However, a good practice for any business is to carefully monitor incoming boxes of merchandise to make sure that your order was fulfilled correctly. That can't happen when the boxes sit where UPS left them by the front door or when the delivery was quickly shoved inside your storeroom.

Before we get to why this practice is costing you money, let's consider the aesthetics of your store with a bunch of boxes lying in the middle of your sales floor. Do you really want customers to be doing a two-step around the boxes as they try to shop? Quickly put the product out or away until the store is closed. If that's not possible, then place the boxes in a spot that's out of the customer's way and preferably out of sight.

You may not even open the box for a while. You check the sender's name and assume it's a certain order you recall making.

Even if you do open the box right away, you're not out of the woods. Opening the box to see what it is and not inventorying the order until later may make you doubt the accuracy of the count when you do get ready to properly stow the merchandise.

After all, with the box open in your storeroom, anyone may have sold a product out of that box or even pilfered one. Make it a priority practice at your store to inventory and store incoming merchandise in a timely manner.

Profitable Retailers know what not inventorying their merchandise as soon as it arrives means for the bottom line: if one vendor a month mistakenly shorts you $100 worth of product at cost, that's $1,200 of profit out of your pocket. If your net operating profit is ten percent, you have to make $12,000 of additional sales just for those "small" mistakes.

Profitable Retailers know there are no small mistakes. When it comes to profitability, these so-called small mistakes are similar to a slow leak in a tire. It may take awhile, but eventually that tire is going to be flat.

The best way to stay on top of incoming merchandise is to have a system – any system – that works for you. Your system may be a computer-based inventory or nothing more complicated than a clipboard with purchase orders hanging on a nail in your store room. It doesn't matter if you adapt someone else's system or invent your own – Profitable Retailers find a system that works for them and then they use it.

Mistakes happen in fulfilling orders, even amongst the most reliable vendors. That's why inventorying and accounting for all merchandise must be a top priority at your store.

The Question: Does your system for inventorying incoming merchandise protect your profits?

50

Ring Up the Profits

Incoming telephone calls to your store are rich with potential. These prospects may have called you because of an ad or other marketing outreach program you've started. Maybe they found your store in the telephone directory, on the Internet, or other business listings. It makes no sense to have spent the dollars required to be seen in the community and then lose the sale because incoming callers were not treated right.

Start off on the right foot by ensuring that the phone is answered promptly – after no more than three rings. You can also start the call off right by having a standardized store greeting so that everyone answers the phone in the same way. Profitable Retailers use a script, since they know that consistency in how the phone is answered is key to the overall customer experience.

Print the script out on a small piece of paper and post it somewhere near the phone. Require your employees to use it. The phone script should be short and to the point. It should always end with the employee's name, not "How may I help you?" This allows a better human connection over the phone. The best script goes like this: "Good [morning, afternoon, evening] and thank you for calling Dynamic Experiences Group, this is Doug."

This is old advice, but so many retail stores still haven't caught on. It does no good to have a script if the greeting is a slurred sentence that customers can't understand, or said so fast they can't understand it. Customers are forming judgments about your store based on how the telephone is answered.

People who call your store want information and answers. These callers don't want to wait until next Tuesday when Pete, your [fill in the blank] expert, comes back from vacation and will be able to return the call.

Profitable Retailers encourage callers to come for a visit. What could be better than having your prospect see the store in action? You want the caller to experience your store firsthand. By getting the customer to your store, you benefit by being able to talk to your prospect one-on-one and get to know the particular needs and goals of the prospect. Make sure your store has a system for scheduling these visits so that your prospect will be expected and handled well. And don't forget to have accurate directions on hand in case the prospect isn't sure how to find the store.

Knowing how your prospect found out about your store is crucial for analyzing your marketing efforts. Few prospects mind answering, "How did you hear about us?" This is a good way to track the effectiveness of your ads, your newsletter, your website, your signage, your listing on the Chamber of Commerce website, or the power of referrals.

The Question: Do you make the most of turning callers into customers?

You Can't Leave the Finances to the Pocket-Protectors

A good accountant is important to any retailer. Profitable Retailers use an accountant to file taxes or create balance sheets and other important financial documents. But they don't need an accountant to tell them how the business is doing.

Profitable Retailers know their expenses, their product costs and margins, and most of all, their profits. One of the biggest mistakes many small retailers make is not having the financial understanding to be profitable. One Profitable Retailer told me the best investment he ever made was taking an entry-level accounting course at the local community college.

Profitable Retailers never confuse sales and profits. I once met a retailer who was so pleased that her sales were up nearly twenty-five percent for the year, but she had no idea how it was impacting her profitability. It's possible she had either increased her advertising expenses or reduced her prices to achieve the sales growth, thus greatly impacting her profits. She could actually have been losing money instead of making money.

Growing sales is important to your bottom line. Growing profits is the ultimate goal. It's critical that you or your accountant provide year-to-date profit and loss statements on a monthly or quarterly basis. Without them, it's like driving a car without a speedometer or fuel gauge. You're going in some direction but you have no idea how fast or how far you can go.

If you don't know your ROA from your P&L, or the differences between assets, liability, and equity, do yourself a favor and sign up for Accounting 101. A good goal is to start off by saying that you're going to understand everything about accounting that you don't understand now. It might just be the difference between profit and loss.

If night school isn't for you, don't overlook your public library or local bookstore for a wealth of information that can help. You can study at your own pace and fill in the gaps in your financial knowledge. The popular series of *Dummies* books even has an *Accounting for Dummies*. If there weren't thousands of people just like you, there wouldn't be the host of books on basic accounting.

Don't be shy about asking questions. Just like any discipline, accounting has its own terms and jargon. When you're talking to your accountant, ask questions; take notes and what may have seemed incomprehensible to you might become clear.

The Question: What can you do to increase your knowledge of accounting?

Keep it Simple

Sometimes the best analysis comes from asking the simplest question. That's why children often have such insightful comments. Their unsophisticated questions cut right to the meat of the issue. Many of us have wanted to put our hands over the mouth of one of our children who ask, "Why is her skin so wrinkled?" or "Where did that man's hair go?"

One of the simplest ways to take a look at your store is to pose two questions to your staff:

- *"What is working?"*

- *"What isn't working?"*

Asking (and answering) those two questions will give you a mass of information about how well your store is operating. The answers don't have to be anything more than a list. In fact, you might pose these questions at a meeting and write the answers on big pieces of paper – one sheet for what's working and one sheet for what's not.

In one store, for example, what's working may be: store newsletter, front window display, new light fixtures, routine for cleaning the store. What's not working may be: how it's decided who works what shifts, inventorying new merchandise, how break times are handled, people's personal property in store room, updating the website.

Posing the questions in this way also presents them in a nonjudgmental way. For example, instead of saying, "I never get my lunch break until 3 o'clock because Joan always gets first choice," all one has to say is "How we decide break times is not working." People and their personalities are removed from it.

When it comes to what's not working, Profitable Retailers know that everything that's attempted may not work. That's why it's a good idea to pause from time to time to examine the systems in place at your store.

Another simple exercise is to keep asking "Why?" until you drill down to the meat of the problem. You might start with, "We don't have enough store traffic." Why? "Because our ads haven't hit yet." Why? "Because we missed the last deadline." Why? "Because we let the deadline get away from us." Why? "Because we weren't paying attention." Why? "Because we were busy running the store." Why? "Because I still haven't learned that I should be working on the store, and not in the store." Why? "Because I'm just now learning how to be a Profitable Retailer." See how well this works?

What other simple questions are there? Here are some more questions to consider:

- *What are we doing?*

- *What should we be doing?*

- *What should we be doing more of?*

- *What should we be doing less of?*

- *What should we do next?*

These simple questions are a great way for Profitable Retailers to sit back and gain some insight into their stores. The questions are so easy – and yet so important – that everyone on your staff will be able to participate in the analysis. Don't rush through the answers. These questions are so broad and simple that an entire meeting could be devoted to each one.

The Question: What simple question should you ask yourself and your employees about your store?

53

The Devil is in the Details
Unless it's Deviled Eggs

One of the best exercises Profitable Retailers can perform is to find one or two things to improve about their store every day. You may start out with major projects – such as noticing your store needs new carpet or a paint job. Eventually, though, you'll notice some smaller details that detract from the appearance of your store. It becomes harder and harder to find something big to correct, which is when you start to see the things you've missed.

This practice is easy to start. You don't even need a budget, and you don't need a lot of time. No one is so busy that they can't take the time to do one thing to improve the appearance of their store each day. After a while, though, Profitable Retailers may want to set aside some money for some larger improvements in their store such as a paint job or new carpeting.

But to get yourself started, think small. For example, most stores I visit have empty sign holders out. Clearly, people working in the store just fail to notice the small details. About half of the stores I visit have left the door to the stockroom open. It's sloppy looking and it takes away from your products and the customer's store experience.

If you're going to put a sign on a locked front door that reads "Out for Lunch" or "Back in 20 Minutes," write down what time you left or what time you'll be back. "Back in 20" means nothing if the customer doesn't know what time you left.

When you sell white or light-colored products, you should sell off your floor model from time-to-time to keep your product fresh and appealing. It's not hard to find some pretty ratty-looking product on sales floors these days.

Here's a small detail that could make your customers say, "Wow!" What would happen if you arrived to open the store and there were customers waiting to come in? Would you walk right by them? Would you explain that you'll be open at 9 a.m. on the dot?

Consider just letting them in the store. By the time you hang up your coat and turn on all the lights, your customer might be ready to pay. Letting customers in your store early is the easiest "Wow!" you can get.

The Question: Does your attention to detail show your customers that they're the most important thing happening in your store?

Making Sure "Easy Come, Easy Go" Doesn't Apply to Your Profits

Unaccounted loss of money or merchandise is a problem for every retailer, regardless of size. Shrinkage occurs because of poorly defined or executed business processes, internal theft, or shoplifting.

What some retailers don't realize, though, is that the losses from internal theft are greater than the losses from shoplifting. That's right – your trusted employees are stealing from you in greater proportion than strangers. Many retailers can tell you heartbreaking stories of employees they trusted like members of the family, who turned out to be thieves.

Economic conditions have contributed to an increase in employee theft. The tight labor market often leaves employers short-staffed and employees by themselves. And more dishonest employees are entering into the workplace because of reduced hiring standards. These factors have combined to create an environment ripe for employee theft. According to the United States Small Business Administration, the financial loss caused by the typical (apprehended) dishonest employee theft is $1,350, while the value of the average amount of merchandise taken by the typical (apprehended) shoplifter is just $196.

Employee theft cuts across the board in retail. It's not only huge stores like Wal-Mart and Nordstrom where a problem exists. It's just plain naïve to believe that employee theft is not a problem – or a potential problem – at your store. Should you consider your business immune to employee theft, think again!

Add to employee theft the losses from shoplifting and you have a huge problem that needs to be addressed in a systematic and realistic way. Although we may never be able to put an end to employee theft or other losses, we can make it harder for both losses to occur. Here are some procedures Profitable Retailers use that may work well in your store:

Develop and adhere to strict processes to receive merchandise and the accompanying paperwork flow. It's easy when boxes arrive to push them aside to deal with later when you're not so busy. Next thing you know, one box gets opened and the rest are ignored for later. Consider, though, that vendors and shipping companies make mistakes and lose products. If a box is opened and not inventoried, you'll miss mistakes, creating shrinkage. Standardizing the receiving process ensures that all steps are followed, including receiving the merchandise and matching it against the packing slip before putting the merchandise on the sales floor.

Give great customer service. That sounds funny, doesn't it? That you should give a shoplifter great customer service? Attention is the last thing shoplifters want. They hate to be waited on and depend on employees who are busy doing other things. There's nothing a shoplifter likes more than a sales associate engrossed in a cell phone conversation or with a nose buried in paperwork. When customers are your number one priority, loss will automatically be reduced.

Shoplifters come in all ages, shapes, sexes, and races. Don't find yourself profiling customers. First of all, it's bad for business. Second, it's bad for society. And three, you'll lose more products because of it. As you scrutinize every movement of the person you're sure is a shady character, the person who least looks the part will be cramming merchandise into a bag. You may have seen shoplifters interviewed on television who depended on the notion that they didn't "look the part." Shoplifters pride themselves on appearing well-dressed and prosperous – they look like solid citizens.

Create policies for how high-value, small items are shown to customers. Most jewelers will only show one piece of jewelry at a time. If you sell small, expensive items, get in the habit of putting one back in the display case before bringing the other out. The products you sell may require you to show two side-by-side. If that's the case, then limit it to two, and ask the customer to decide which two to compare.

In addition, you must train your staff to be aware of times with customers when their full attention is mandatory. What are situations when shoplifting may be likely to occur? When small, expensive items are out of a display case, it's all too easy for a sales associate to turn away for a moment to answer the phone or talk to another customer.

Internal theft is a sad but real fact of life for retailer. The biggest mistake most retailers make is that they can't believe that any of their employees would steal from them. Statistics tell us otherwise. Security experts estimate that as many as thirty percent of all employees steal, and that another sixty percent will steal if given sufficient motive and opportunity.

The best deterrents to internal theft are well-defined policies like making daily bank deposits, keeping back doors locked and alarmed during the day, not allowing employees to ring up their own purchases, limiting the amount of bags an employee can bring to work, etc.

Constant and open auditing. Every day the owner or manager should review the store's sales from the day before to look for signs like excessive refunds, refunds without accompanying receipts, or steep unauthorized discounts. A high number of no sale transactions that open a cash drawer can be a sign an employee is taking cash from customers, not ringing it in the register, and then opening the drawer to remove the cash when the customer leaves. Audit openly so employees know that you review the day's receipts. You can tell your staff you like to review the information so you get a good feel for the business, especially after a day or an evening off.

Profitable Retailers know that their jobs as owners and managers are to keep honest people honest. A good employee could be tempted one time or another to steal something, but having good store practices in place will keep them from acting on this urge. The fear of being caught is a good motivator to not steal. Dishonest people will steal from you and the best you can hope for is that they get greedy, which every thief does, and then they'll get caught.

The Question: Do you have policies in place to combat shrinkage and other internal losses?

Say What? Projecting a Positive Image on the Phone

You might not think of telephone interaction with customers as part of your marketing efforts, but it is – and can be just as important as advertising, news releases, flyers or brochures. Profitable Retailers know that every time someone from their store speaks with a customer, that conversation is forming, maintaining, or changing an impression of their store.

The mere act of answering the phone can increase or decrease your store's appeal. It's easy in the rush of the day to give responses that may be truthful, but don't create a positive and professional image. Here are some samples:

"Pete's still at lunch." If it's 3 p.m., your customer might conjure an image of Pete on his third martini. It very well may be the case that Pete worked nonstop until 2:55 and then ran out for a sandwich. Rather than supplying the casual and specific information, consider saying instead: "Pete's not available right now. My name is Ron. May I help you?"

"Ann hasn't come in yet." This is the same situation as being "still at lunch." The problem is the word "yet." To most ears "yet" is the same as "late." Just like Pete's lunch in the first example, Ann's workday may not start until mid-morning, but the customer doesn't know that. An improved answer is the same: "Ann's not available right now. My name is Ron. May I help you?"

"Gee, I don't know where he is right now. He was just here." What kind of place are you running there, anyway? In the hubbub of a busy day, it's very possible that the boss could slip out to go to the bank, to an appointment, or elsewhere, making him or her unavailable to speak on the phone. Rather than appearing not to know what's going on, it's safer to go with the standard reply: "Dan's not available right now. My name is Ron. May I help you?"

"She went home early." Want to make a customer angry? Tell him that the employee who was supposed to handle something or return his phone call "went home early." It's a surefire way to irritate any customer. There may be a very good reason why a person "went home early" on a particular day, but mostly this explanation conjures up an image of calling it quits to relax.

"He's at the doctor right now." Is he dying? What's wrong with him? How come he's at the doctor? Personal information about the whereabouts of an employee – "He's at his lawyer's" or "She's having her teeth cleaned" or "He had to go pick up his boy from school" are best left unsaid. If the employee wants to share the information later with coworkers or customers, that's another matter. But respect the privacy of your employees by keeping their commitments private.

"He's with a customer right now." As the saying goes, "What am I? Chopped liver?" When you tell one customer that someone is unavailable because the person is with a customer, you're implying that first customer is more important than the caller. One customer doesn't want to feel as if he or she is less important than another.

"She's busy right now. Can you call back?" Customers don't want to be characterized as a nuisance who is trying to intrude on someone's busy day. The problem with telling a customer to call back is that they may never do that. That customer may decide that they don't really want to visit your store, or place an order, or apply for a job, or recommend a friend to you. No business should ever ask a customer to call back.

The Question: Have you trained your employees to answer the phone correctly? Have you trained them to respond appropriately?

Basic Actions Bring
Unbasic Profits

Most retail owners have read a pile of books and magazine articles about improving sales and how business is conducted. In fact, many Profitable Retailers could write their own books on what works to increase sales. Yet just like knowing which foods are healthy or that daily exercise is good, it's harder to put into practice the wise business tenets that everyone knows work. Here are three that could use extra attention:

Follow up. Business is lost every workday because someone somewhere didn't follow up on sales leads or a customer request. A prospect may ask, "Can you have someone call me about the availability of this product?" That's a direct request for a follow-up. Don't ignore it or forget it or think, "Oh well, she's just shopping around. We need serious prospects." Make the call – it's the best way to encourage more business.

Sometimes a customer's request for follow-up won't be as direct. When a customer says, "I'm thinking of buying a new sewing machine after Christmas," that customer is giving you a go-ahead to follow up. Give a quick phone call. Your customer won't think you're pushy. Your customer will be glad for the reminder. Maybe a customer mentions a friend or relative who would enjoy your store and its merchandise. That's a green light for you to ask for contact information. Don't lose the referral by ignoring it. At the very least, extend an invitation for the friend or family member to come in for a visit. Pass along a business card. That's a way to follow up, too.

Know your product. Sure, you've been selling this merchandise for twenty years, and you're an expert. If a customer asks you about new trends in the products you offer, can you answer? A customer might ask, "Why is this one so much more expensive than that one?" Would you be able to explain the price difference to that customer in a manner that's not just generalities like "That's a better product"?

A variety of people at your store need to be able to handle different customer requests. More than one person should be able to greet a customer and give them information. Telling a prospective customer, "You need to talk to Jason. He'll be in on Friday, if you're really interested" is no way to make a sale.

You can improve the performance of your staff and your bottom line by trying some role-playing scenarios dealing with customer issues. Even top-notch salespeople still practice their craft. In fact, top-notch salespeople are the ones who continue to train and improve their own performance.

Don't knock the competition. Saying negative things about the store across town or in the next town doesn't make them look bad; it makes *you* look bad. You might think you're creating a great competitive advantage for your store ("They don't offer half the products we have"), but you're only making the customer uncomfortable. If you want to differentiate why spending money with you is better than doing it with the competition, stress your strengths not their weaknesses.

When you talk about the competition, keep it factual and keep your emotion out of it as much as possible. A customer might say, "I bought this camera at another store…" That's not an invitation to roll your eyes. That's not an invitation to interrupt with a sarcastic comment like, "That was your first mistake." For all you know, that customer might finish the sentence by saying, "And I want to buy one just like it for my wife."

If it turns out that the customer wants something that you can't do – like repair or exchange – explain why in a straightforward manner. Think of the person standing in front of you as presenting an opportunity to get a new customer and react accordingly.

The Question: How can you use these basic actions to become more profitable?

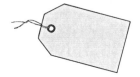

Into Action

Winston Churchill once said, "I never worry about action, but only about inaction." Action *is* the key. In reading this book, I hope it has spurred ideas, thoughts, and opportunities. I hope it has challenged your way of thinking and the way you run your business. I hope that you will now do some things differently and continue doing other things the way you always have. Most important, I hope you have taken some action to date and have committed yourself to doing even more.

If you are not meeting your sales goal, then do something about it. If you're not generating enough profits, do something about it. If you don't have the staff you want, do something about it. If your life isn't the way you want it, do something about it. Take action. I believe that the greatest limitation to our success lies within us. It's not "them," your competitors, your customers, or your employees who hold you back. It's you. You can be as successful and as profitable as you choose. First make the choice, then take the action. The profits will follow.

I wish you luck on your journey to becoming a Profitable Retailer. The road is filled with laughter and tears, peace and fear, and trials and tribulations. But along the way you will also find financial reward and personal satisfaction, two things worth the trip. I hope to see you on the way. Keep it fun.

About the Authors

Doug Fleener

Doug is president and managing partner of the Lexington, MA- based retail consulting firm Dynamic Experiences Group, LLC and is the author of numerous articles on the topics of retail, employee motivation, and customer service. As the Director of Retail for Bose Corporation, Doug grew the Retail Direct Group from four to one hundred stores. Under his leadership, the Bose retail stores became one of the pre-eminent specialty retailers in consumer electronics, known for their highly customer-focused approach and multimedia Bose Music Theater Show. Doug's expertise has been cited in *The Washington Post, Entrepreneur Magazine, The Christian Science Monitor,* and *Shopping Centers Today.* His articles on the retail experience have appeared in *The Boston Business Journal, North American Retail Dealers Association, Photo Marketing Association Magazine,* and *Cape Cod Business.* He also publishes two widely read newsletters, *The Retail Experience* and *The Profitable Retailer.*

Doug currently lives in Lexington, Massachusetts, with his wife and two young daughters, where in his free time he barbecues while listening to Jimmy Buffet.

Doug can be contacted at doug@dougfleener.com.

Patricia Luebke

Patricia Luebke is a New York City-based consultant with more than thirty years marketing experience. Her specialty is small businesses and providing useful information to help these companies become stronger and more profitable. She has written dozens of articles on business and the fundamentals of marketing practice including pieces on media relations, advertising, trade shows, websites, newsletters, logos, direct mail, and customer communications. Her articles always include business insights, marketing tips, and practical ideas all designed to empower entrepreneurs to become better marketers.

Contact Us

We'd love to hear your success stories. If after reading this book your sales and profits have increased, we would love to hear about it. We also welcome your comments, suggestions, or topics that you'd like to see in our next *Profitable Retailer* book. Send those success stories and comments to doug@theprofitableretailer.com.

Have Doug present at your next company meeting or tradeshow. Need a fun and powerful speaker for your next event? While some business speakers bore audiences to tears – Doug turns every event into an experience. His audience-interactive speaking programs are designed to teach retailers, small and large, how to deliver the kinds of extraordinary shopping experiences that differentiate retailers from their competition. Sometimes wacky, but always informative, Doug gets audiences thinking differently about the way they approach their business. His insights into customer behavior and employee satisfaction go against the grain of traditional retail practices, much like his taste in shirts. Read about Doug's programs at www.dougfleener.com or call us at 866-535-6331.

Have us help you grow your sales and profits. Contact us to discuss how we might work together to create the success you deserve. We offer a host of services and programs for retailers of all sizes. Learn more at www.dynamicexperiencesgroup.com or call us at 866-535-6331.

Sign up for our FREE monthly newsletters,
The Profitable Retailer and *The Retail Experience,*
at www.retailnewsletters.com.

Order this book in bulk and save. Companies and
tradeshows can help create more Profitable Retailers
among their customers and members by sharing this book
with them. We do offer discounts on bulk purchases.
Contact us at 866-535-6331 or email us at
info@theprofitableretailer.com to discover how.